Memories of
THE AIR WAR
IN EAST ANGLIA

Memories of THE AIR WAR IN EAST ANGLIA

A Nostalgic Tribute to the US 8th Air Force in
Norfolk, Suffolk, Cambridgeshire & Beyond

MARTIN BOWMAN

HALSGROVE

First published in Great Britain in 2009

British Library Cataloguing-in-Publication Data
A CIP record for this title is available from the British Library

ISBN 978 1 84114 938 7

HALSGROVE
Halsgrove House,
Ryelands Industrial Estate,
Bagley Road, Wellington, Somerset TA21 9PZ
Tel: 01823 653777   Fax: 01823 216796
email: sales@halsgrove.com

Part of the Halsgrove group of companies
Information on all Halsgrove titles is available at: www.halsgrove.com

Printed and bound by Grafiche Flaminia, Italy

CONTENTS

ACKNOWLEDGEMENTS

The author and publisher extend grateful thanks to the following people: Paula Allen; David & Lorinda Crow; John Gilbert; Steve Gotts; the late Peter Haining for permission to use Philipp's Miller's illustrations; Paul Knight; Pete Howard; John McClane; Seward M. 'Mort' Meinstma; Judge Ben Smith Jr; Nigel McTeer; Ernest E. 'Ernie' Russell; Cal Sloan; Roy West; Paul Wilson.

INTRODUCTION

When American servicemen began arriving in East Anglia it created a culture shock the like of which war-weary Britons had never seen before or since. The 'Yanks', or the 'GIs' as they were more popularly known, found life in East Anglia equally as bemusing – both on and off base. Though America was only just emerging from isolationism, and thousands of the new arrivals were from the backwoods and the boondocks and the multitude of small towns in vast agricultural regions of the Mid West, they found Britain, with its black-out, poor food, lack of central heating and other privations and shortages brought about by almost three years of war, hard to take. Few knew what to expect. Those that had read about Britain in popular fiction held romantic notions of castles and country houses, but these were quickly dispelled, especially when the stark realities of life on remote air bases in Norfolk and Suffolk, Cambridgeshire and Essex began to take effect.

On 22 February 1942 VIIIth Bomber Command was formerly activated in England under the command of Major General Ira C. Eaker. He and his chiefs in Washington believed that the B-17 Flying Fortresses and B-24 Liberators, heavily armed so as not to need escort fighters, could, in broad daylight, penetrate even the strongest defences without high losses. They also sought the 'pickle barrel' bombing accuracy that bombardiers had performed in the clear skies of Texas and the southern States. But by September losses were on the increase. The RAF and even some in the USAAF were of the opinion that bombing in daylight was suicidal – as it was on occasions – but the Americans never faltered. US escort fighters arrived, albeit late in the war, and by spring 1944 the P-51 Mustang was escorting the US 'heavies' to Berlin and back. Ultimately, the 'round the clock' bombing by the RAF at night and the Eighth Air Force by day, helped to achieve victory

Stirring deeds of these gladiators of the air filled the newspapers and magazines of the period. They were crystallized in the minds of the population with movies such as William Wyler's wartime epic 'Memphis Belle', a poignant feature screened on both sides of the Atlantic, about the lives of a B-17 crew who flew that particular ship on 25 missions.

Opposite page: Duxford based P-47 Thunderbolt in 'Chequerboard' markings – the type flown by Ernie Russell, 'a brand-new' 21-year old' in the 78th Fighter Group in WW2. Ernie was in combat for eight months and his 64th and last mission from Duxford in May 1944 completed his tour of 201 hours and 21 minutes.

THE AIR WAR IN EAST ANGLIA

In the 21st century this immortal period of Anglo-American history is still being commemorated, with new films, books and magazine articles about the period, and with celebrations for the returning US veterans and the English families who had opened their hearts and homes to them so long ago.

Those Second World War years are recalled here by a cast of characters no movie director could ever hope to assemble. They tell of laughter, friendship, death, fear, exhilaration, stupidity, superstitions, discipline and indiscipline, lust and love, respect, disrespect, and outrage. Also of course the sheer horrors faced mission after mission by the 'boys in the sky', together with the personal deprivations experienced by the British men, women and children. These are their memories.

Martin W. Bowman
Norwich, England

PROLOGUE

'We boarded our carriage for a long ride. The weather in the late July of 1943 was miserable in the Scottish Lowlands. A cold drizzle misted out of patches of low clouds below an overcast sky; the 'carriages' were not well heated and the damp cold seeped through my light uniform. We had left summer in Florida to meet winter in Scotland and it was still July. Settled uncomfortably into our seats, too miserable even to talk, the only sound in our compartment was that of steel wheels rolling on steel rails. But there was no 'clackity-clack'.

Our route took us south through the low, rolling and barren hills of southern Scotland, so I hunkered down and began to take in the landscape. I could understand why the Scots were said to be dour. One could not help but be depressed by the weather and the barren, almost desolate, treeless landscape with stone fences that climbed the hills like so many tent caterpillars marking off each grass pasture as an independency. At intervals, ancient, cold, gray stone houses with thatch roofs dotted the dreary loneliness of the hills. Often there was an attached stone barn. Seldom did I see a Scotsman, only shaggy sheep browsing contentedly in the enclosures and they seemed unconcerned with the bleakness of their surroundings. Regardless of the damp, chilly weather, the rain and my summer uniforms, I was thrilled to be where I had never thought I'd be in Scotland and on my way to England. The last of my ancestors to depart the British Isles left before the early 1700s.

Gradually, the landscape began to change and soon we were in agricultural East Anglia, a beautiful rolling and fertile area that greatly resembled the rich Black Prairies back home in north-east Mississippi. We began to see clusters of brick and stone houses built around ancient stone churches with tall, slender, steeples in the little villages; all appeared to be grimy, or was it the weather? The villages became more frequent and larger the further south we travelled. Finally, there were continuous blocks of 'row houses', stacked like dominoes, side by side; obviously, we were approaching a major population centre. Only when we were pulling into Liverpool Street Station did I grasp that the row houses were in London. Liverpool Street

Station was a bleak, but famous, rusty steel behemoth. Coated with grim and ashes from the coal burning locomotives, it was all shades of grey a wartime England had neither the time nor wherewithal to clean up and paint. In contrast, the brass, or copper, no matter where, always looked as if it had just been polished. At any given time smoke from the numerous steam locomotives drifting across the platforms mixing with London's mists and ghost-like there was always a bustling crowd of soldiers, sailors, airmen and civilians, all rushing into, or out off a compartment and out of the station at once. The skylights, long since obscured with soot and dirt, let in little sunlight so the station resembled a giant, poorly lighted cave. The very size of the great cavernous station, wreathed in a steamy mist from the numerous steam engines, impressed me. But the acrid smoke made my eyes smart and insulted my nostrils. Nonetheless, the long concrete platforms were bustling with people hurrying hither and thither.

All was new to me, the country, the transportation, the people, everything. Uniforms were everywhere. The good looking blue uniforms of the Royal Air Force. The slightly baggy, almost shoddy, but serviceable wool khaki uniforms and hob nailed boots of the British Army. The neat looking-uniforms of the Women's' Auxiliary and a few kilts. Servicemen in Polish and Free French uniforms with their strange looking hats were scattered through the crowd. The civilians, men and women, had on warm clothes, but most were seedy. After all, the British had been at war for four years and clothing was rationed. Every one was scurrying about, head down, rushing like they were about to miss a train. The lack of eye-to-eye contact was disconcerting and struck me as a Southerner I had yet to learn that my distant kinsmen are uncommunicative with strangers. It just hadn't sunk in to my awareness - yet. Only a wizened little man in a ragged coat looked at me directly and that was because he wanted to sell his big bunches of black grapes; the only grapes I ever saw in England during the war. I could have spent the afternoon just watching the diverse people in Liverpool Street Station; London is truly a melting pot. Back home we would do the same thing in the small towns on Saturday night. But we were denied that pleasure.

Finally, we were directed to our train, which we boarded and shortly a shrill whistle blew. A man came down the platform, slamming compartment doors and the train glided out of the station. The engineer eased the train out of the station with no squealing and clanging of metal on metal, no banging about. It was as though the train had fluid drive. I could not get over how smoothly the train got under way. Soon we were out of the station passing dingy houses with dirty windows and sooty chimneys on the northwest side of London.

We craned our necks looking for the bomb damage shown in the papers and newsreels back home; to my surprise, I saw none. However, in the haze, high over the city, I could barely discern the outlines of great sausage-shaped barrage balloons floating calmly in the sky. I knew that they were tethered by deadly steel cables that were invisible and that other steel cables hung down from them like the tentacles of a giant jellyfish, which purpose was to trap prey.

On the outskirts of London we were soon passing two storey brick houses with neat gardens and boxes full of flowers in the windows. Train stations flashed by. Many of the names on the stations were familiar; some resonated in my memory and reminded me that we were in

A HITCH IN TIME

Pin-ups such as this followed the American servicemen from the United States and became familiar icons throughout Britain, appearing on playing cards, as nose art on aircraft and decorating the Nissen huts and mess halls on airfields. A number have been included throughout this book.

England, the source of the names for most small towns in Mississippi. The few vehicles on the narrow Macadam roadways were mostly military and the very few English cars were small and ancient looking. The countryside was lush, green, rolling and peaceful – where was the war?

Late in the afternoon after a long tiresome trip the train pulled into Shrewsbury (Shrozebury to the locals). My Welsh ancestors, the Roberts and wife's, the Evans, would have been happy for me. I soon came to know that Shrewsbury, which is on the border of England and Wales, is an ancient British town with a very long and troubled history.

'Six-bys' were waiting to pick us up and to give us a sight seeing trip, sans guide, through Shrewsbury and a long ride through the country. The English roads we travelled in were very old, made for horse-drawn wagons and carriages, not for military vehicles, and as such they were narrow, winding and had the nasty habit of almost becoming a single lane when passing through little communities. When the sun came out at last it illuminated the beauty of the English countryside. We passed one old pub that I would get to know.

In a little while we turned into a tree lined lane onto the US Air Force base at Atcham, a small English farm village about four miles southeast of Shrewsbury. Our stay was so short that I can never remember going into the village. The airbase was set up to train replacement pilots for the three operational P-47 fighter groups in the 8th Fighter Command. My greatest disappointment at Atcham was that I did not get to fly that most beautiful and graceful of airplanes, the Spitfire. I was scheduled to check out in one of the 'Spit Vs' but before I could complete the ground checks I was on my way to a fighter group. In due course it was down to the railroad station and on to London. There we took a '6-by' to another train station and boarded a train on our way to Duxford.

The train ride from Atcham to a foggy London train station made for a long day but the beautiful green and gold of the English countryside through which we passed more than made up for it. We had a short stop in London and then boarded another train, which on a big board said 'Cambridge'. The ride was shorter this time, again through beautiful countryside that was dotted with little villages. The time passed slowly but finally, the train squealed to a stop, without a single bump or bang, at a typical, small railway station in the English countryside. The station sign was marked, WHITTLESFORD - where was Duxford? Time would tell that it was the next little village to the west, on the east side of the 'aerodrome'. Whittlesford was typical of small rural communities in England that were fortunate to have a 'whistle stop' train station. Always clean and neat, even though sooty and slightly rundown, all the train stations seemed to be alike: raised concrete platforms, or landings, on both sides of the track to service both coming and going traffic. Frequently the two sides were connected by an overhead walkway to a ticket office and there was a waiting room with a ticket office on one side. Often, an iron or wooden fence separates the station from the nearby road. The rolling countryside surrounding the station was beautiful and yellow with the maturing wheat. The station was only a short distance from the 'Red Lion'. For some reason, I can't remember going to it.

Whittlesford and Duxford were distinctively rural England. The scattered houses along the road were invariably brick and had that wartime drab and deeply weathered appearance. The

Kings College, Cambridge. It was in Cambridge that Ernie Russell got his hair cut and went pub crawling.

Ernie Russell on his return to Duxford in 2008.

colour of the brick was obscured by soot from myriad wood and coal fires. A few of the cottages had thatch roofs but most were quaint old houses with moss covered tile roofs. Typically English, some fronted the road while others had a small 'yard' not much bigger than the flower box that hung beneath the windows. Flowers grew in profusion is the small spaces. Wooden houses are a rarity in the English countryside; the forests had been cut long ago so lumber was rare and expensive. But English homes were built to last and the typical Englishman is inordinately proud of his abode no matter how humble. I distinctly remember being lectured by a very pretty young lady in a proper girl's school that I, being American, probably would not appreciate the fact that her family lived in a thatched-roof cottage some four hundred years old. Some cottage!

Minutes after we passed through Whittlesford large red brick buildings began to appear through a row of hedges on our right, the north. The '6-by' slowed and turned right through a gate in the hedge. Another right turn brought us to a circle and we stopped in front of a beautiful, red-brick building with fan glass windows framing the entrance above the door - the Duxford Officers Club. And this was war? We didn't know how lucky we were; most of our classmates were assigned to temporary bases; living for the most part in Quonset huts and the perpetual mud of recently constructed airfields that dotted the East Anglia countryside.

As soon as the truck came to a stop in front of that magnificent building, we jumped down and followed an enlisted man into the club. The foyer met my expectations, airy, open with high ceilings and comfortable chairs scattered around. After a short walk down a hallway, we lined up in front of an office to receive our room assignments and bed linens. Now to find our new 'digs'. The room assignments were alphabetic and Ernie Lang and my good friend Macie V. Marlowe an old classmate from RTU, were assigned to rooms near to me. Marlowe was a tall, lanky, somewhat bleary-eyed tousled haired Virginian, who was just short of being handsome. He had been married to a strikingly beautiful girl only a short time before we embarked for overseas. Most had been assigned choice rooms in the main, steam-heated, two-story BOQ attached to the Officers Club. The billeting officer had run out of spaces in the main building and had assigned us to rooms in a detached, temporary, wooden, barracks building just west of the main Officers Club, which some thought were the least desirable quarters, as they were unheated and not in the mess. However, we had the advantage of our own private room and they beat the huge, corrugated metal half culverts called 'Quonset huts' or the tents in which, many of our classmates were living.

Duxford had had a long history as a fighter station before the 78th Fighter Group arrived there in early 1943. It had been an early Royal Flying Corps airfield prior to World War One and we were not the first Americans to be there; a unit of the US Army's fledgling flying service was stationed there during WWI, the 'War to end all wars'. After that conflict Duxford again became a permanent Royal Flying Corps, later Royal Air Force, station. The RAF flew early model Spitfires from Duxford during the Battle of Britain. Spitfire squadrons stationed at Duxford included those of the uncompromising Douglas Bader and his cohorts who battered the Luftwaffe flying early Mark Hurricanes and Spitfires. One squadron carried WZ markings.

My 84th Fighter Squadron carried the same markings and I connect with the Battle of Britain every time I see a Spitfire with WZ markings emblazoned on its fuselage.

Duxford was an elite station that housed many RAF flying units. Finally, in the 1970s it became the Imperial War Museum with a spectacular collection of aircraft. Our British cousins take great pride in documenting their history and in the nineteen nineties, the British gave generously again, to build a magnificent structure to house American aircraft - the American Air Museum.'

Ernest E. Russell, adapted from *A Mississippi Fighter Pilot in WWII*

Reflected glory. B-17 'Mary Alice' seen through the window of the American Air Museum at the Imperial War Museum, Duxford.

A pin-up album made by a GI from a B-24 bomb bay door in 1945 at Wendling in Norfolk and given to seven-year-old John Gilbert. This album contained many of the pin ups featured throughout this book.

A GLIMPSE OF THE PAST

'IS YOUR JOURNEY REALLY NECESSARY?

'My first taste of austerity travel on the railways of Britain came the day following our arrival in Scotland. The date was 18th August and the newspapers were full of the first American air raid on France. Late that evening we marched down from Bellahouston Park and loaded our duffle into a long, dirty troop train. We did not know how long the journey was to be, or where we were going but we did know that we would be sitting up eight men to a compartment throughout the night.

As the train pulled out of the station the sky was growing dark and we looked out of the windows curiously, noting with interest each feature of the hilly, quiet countryside of Lanarkshire. But it soon blackened and as we strained our eyes through the windows we could see nothing, not even a single light. It was like a continuous ride in an endless tunnel and it was vastly impressive. This was our first experience with the blackout. We marvelled at its completeness.

A glimpse of the past as a steam engine powers along the tracks on the present-day North Norfolk Railway. Such a sight would have been familiar to US airmen.

The compartment became hot and uncomfortable and sprawled and snoring bodies soon made it almost unbearable. One by one the men moved out into the passage and lay down on the arty floor to sleep. I found that the next car forward was an empty baggage car and spread my shelter-half on the floor. When I awoke the next morning, stiff and bruised, I found the floor of the car covered with other sleeping soldiers. We were at Ely - high up on a hill overlooking the flat farmland stood the ancient cathedral.

"Ely! Where the hell is that?" someone asked. I drew back in my memory and scrawled a rough map of England on an envelope. "It's just about here," I said "and I can't figure out why we are going though Ely. I thought we were headed for the south of England."

The countryside flew past and more familiar names of unfamiliar places flashed by. Newmarket, Bury St. Edmunds - Ipswich! We stopped at Ipswich for some time and then moved off again. Finally the train drew into a little country siding and the sign said Wickham Market!

Above: *'Ely, where the hell is that?'*

Right: *Newmarket.*

Here we were then. Who ever heard of Wickham Market? New York, Halifax, Glasgow, Wickham Market! That was probably the first train in the history of England that had gone non-stop from Glasgow to Wickham Market, Suffolk but trains were doing many strange things in those memorable days. And we were to experience even stranger things than that during the following two years.'

Is Your Journey Really Necessary? **Robert S. Arbib Jr.**

DISS

'...*On June 9th, both men and equipment returned to the railroad station from where the first of several trains set out for the small East Anglian town of Diss, to be trucked the last five miles to their final destination, Thorpe Abbotts in the county of Norfolk...*'

Century Bombers. In June 1943 the 100th Bomb Group began moving from Podington to their permanent wartime home in Norfolk. Diss railway station today is not much different to when the GIs arrived and later queued on the platforms for London Liverpool Street.

Orders were issued today from HQ stating that Harleston would be 'Off Limits' to all personnel from this Station because the Colored boys had taken it over. Diss was removed from the 'Off Limits' list even though the Negroes were still there. Of course the white boys had trouble the first night...'

Sergeant Vernon Sheedy, 100th Bomb Group at Thorpe Abbotts.

Diss Station today.

CHRISTMAS IN SUFFOLK

'In America Christmas is the most festive holiday of the year and it is a family affair at which children are always in evidence. You just can't properly celebrate Christmas without children around - without Christmas trees and Santa Claus and presents and ice cream, cake and candy! I went around East Anglia that Christmas, visiting a few of the many celebrations that were being held all that week... Up at Honington, on the estate of the Duke of Grafton, all the children from the orphans' home housed on the Duke's estate were invited to the party... At the hospital at Botesdale there was an even larger party, for here all the children of the neighbouring villages had been invited... At Bury St. Edmunds 1,500 children swarmed the largest hall in town for an afternoon of riotous entertainment and at Ipswich there was a similar party for 1,100 more. At some airfields Santa Claus arrived from the sky in a Flying Fortress and at other camps they appeared in the inevitable jeep. At Kettering there was a special party for six children who had somehow been left out of the first party for seven hundred. At Hull there were plays and pantomimes at parties where each child was adopted by an American "pal," while at Bedford the American soldiers were "buddies," and at Colchester the military police entertained ninety children - all of them with fathers who were prisoners of war...'

The Children Of Britain, Robert S. Arbib Jr

SOME THINGS NEVER CHANGE

'Travel around Britain by train was a confusing proposition to the foreign soldier. Not only were the stations unmarked but the station porters who called their names were almost unintelligible to us....I loved to ride on those trains, though they angered me and tried my patience every

'Travel around Britain by train was a confusing proposition to the foreign soldier.'

time. When I was riding the LNER I was certain that this, of all the railways I had ever seen, was the worst. And certainly the Great Western seemed no better. But when we thought about the incredible conditions under which railways were operating in those days, we forgave them. There was the time on the LNER when a lucky bomb had split the centre of an embankment between Chelmsford and Shenfield just ahead of a train. It took three days to fish that locomotive out of the hole with cranes. Everyone said, *"Why don't they just blow the thing up and fill in the hole*?" But every locomotive was needed and they worked on it night and day for thee days and shuttled passengers around the obstacle by bus.

There were the trains that came into Peterborough North and the connecting train left from Peterborough East, a mile away through the town, just twenty minutes later and no way to get there but to run, dragging your baggage behind you like a mule hitched to a balky plough.

There was the time in the train going out to Watford when I closed my eyes and dozed off to be suddenly awakened by an ominous roar, to find everyone else crouched on the floor. Showing my usual lightning reaction to danger, I froze where I was and the buzz bomb passed overhead to crash a mile away. Brave, these Yanks. Don't know what fear is!

There was the train in Scotland that got completely bogged down somewhere between Loch Lomond and the Glasgow station, when I had just one hour to catch another train to Gourock to meet a third train that was taking an Air Force squadron to King's Cliffe, on which I was to be escorting officer. My flight to catch that last train will ever be a nightmare in my mind, involving a jump from a crawling train, a run for half a mile along the track, a slow tram-car into town, the last bus to Gourock and then another mile run to the pier... just in time to swing aboard the already-moving troop train to King's Cliffe.

Yes, train travel in England was fun those days. Is that a grey hair I see, just above my wrinkled brow?'

Robert S. Arbib Jr.

Big Ben and the statue of Boudicca, London.

CANDY FOR THE CHILDREN

'At one time during the voyage [to Britain] the British crew had to turn the great liner at a 90-degree angle to keep from being hit by a torpedo. So we were told. We travelled from Scotland to London by train. Along the way we gave chocolate and candy to the little children who came up to the train on our various stops. GI K rations were the order of the day. We counted ourselves lucky to get a few cigarettes in the rations. Part of the train trip was at night and we had to keep the curtains of the train drawn. The blackout was of course in force. From London to Bushey Park near the Tudor palace of Hampton Court, ten miles or so from the capital. Our first night there the air raid sirens went off and all the newcomers ran to the protective trenches. After that we just made sure we had our 'dog-tags' on and slid under our cots. Not much of a memory of England.'

'Eisenhower's Sweethearts' Helen M. Meyer

MORE RAILWAY MEMORIES

'There, up ahead of me, is a railway station with a troop train patiently waiting for the shuttle boats to bring our Group ashore. The train itself is much smaller than those that cruise the vast distances across the States. In fact the passenger cars are almost toy-like by comparison, but even though much smaller these cars do have some advantages over ours. The first obvious difference is the boarding. Rather than entering at the front or rear of the car, all we had to do was open one of the many doors and step into the small compartment, which had opposing bench-like seats. At the far end of the compartment was a sliding door that provided access to a long corridor running the length of the car. The train station itself was built on a level with the train right up to a few inches of the train. So entering was both easy and rapid. Soon we were under way, slowly easing out of the station. ...On the rails southward, we rocketed along, occasionally slowing, often hearing the rather haunting sound of our train's whistle as it warned of our approach across roads. As we passed the road, we could see gates closed to prevent bicycles, pedestrians, or an occasional vehicle from crossing. It appeared that these gates were opened and closed manually. No automatic equipment here. ...Naturally there was no luxury of a dining car (if any did exist)...'

From the Diary of Will Lundy, a GI stationed at Shipdham, Norfolk

Always carry your gas mask!

The former airfield at Rackheath, is hidden beneath an industrial site, seen from the air today.

THE RAILWAY AT RACKHEATH

'The engines vary in size from little play things to big ones about 3/4 the size of ours The English coaches are built much the same as ours except that the steps are about 4 feet high and all the stations have raised platforms. The under-carriage is light with 4 wheels at each end and very light springs as well as wheels. The insides of the coaches aren't unlike ours but are narrower and can be cut in two by a door in the middle. Capacity, 48 men. Some coaches we saw were in separate compartments with access only from the outside. Certain ones were designated as "smoking" or "non-smoking".). The freight cars are a different story. They're only about one-fourth the size of ours – twelve feet long and four feet high - and remind me of little mining cars except for their high carriage and springs. They have very small capacity, and the trains don't seem very long altho' some of the engines are fairly large. The box cars are round-roofed and look like a portable hog-house with straight sides - a crude analogy but an apt one.'

Ralph H. Elliott, American pilot at Rackheath, Norfolk

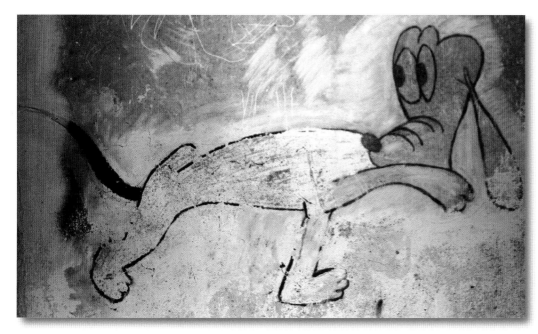

A cartoon picture of Pluto found on a wall at Rackheath, former US airfield.

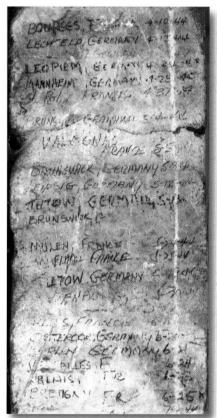

A list of missions flown over Europe in 1944, found on a wall at Rackheath, former US airfield.

FIRST CLASS GREAT YARMOUTH

'A decision was made for all of us to take a train ride to the coastal vacation resort of Great Yarmouth, 20 miles east of Norwich. I insisted that I buy the tickets. I approached the ticket window asking the agent for six tickets to Great Yarmouth. He gave me a set of tickets, which I paid for. When I got back with the family, they almost had a fit; the agent had given me second-class tickets. I thought nothing of it but I was quickly informed that officers only travel first class. I insisted it made no difference to me, but Mr. Colman and the others were more insistent than ever. They finally convinced me that it would be an insult to the Officer corps and an embarrassment to them if I did not exchange them for first class. After complying with their requests, we boarded the train for a most pleasant ride and wonderful day at the seashore and on the boardwalk. Of course none of us went swimming.'

John McClane Jr., navigator

FIRST CLASS TO GREAT YARMOUTH

'No tickets now at 14-bob-round-trip. …You waited on the platform for the train to pull in from Norwich, buying a *Daily Express, Sketch, 'Mail, Post,* or *Illustrated.* Then you read the signs, *"There'll Always Be Mazawattee Tea"* and watched a farmer herd two goats off the train through

'There'll Always be Mazawattee Tea.'

the passengers. And you looked over the local civilians, the British officers, and the scores of American airman, a few of them with all their gear starting the trip back to the States. Local trains from Swaffham and Watton arrived with school-kids in shorts and high wool stockings, clutching their books like the school-kids in all countries. You sat in the compartment and slept most of the way. That is you sat when there was a seat, one of the eight that could be crowded into each compartment. Again you read the signs in the train…"If danger seems imminent, lie on the floor" advised the poster next to the water-colour of the cathedral. "It is *dangerous* for passengers to put their heads out of carriage windows" warned the message over the door with the window you opened by working the heavy leather strap.'

'48 TO LONDON' 1943 from the 359th Fighter Group History

A BREAK FROM EAST ANGLIA - LONDON 1944

'Forty-eight hour passes were not easy to come by, but about once a month we could get one, especially if the weather was bad. For me and for most of my friends, there was only one destination: London. We went to the nearby towns, such as Cambridge, for an evening, but few of us were sophisticated enough to appreciate what the university city and rural England offered; and perhaps they weren't anymore ready for us than we were for them. So, to London we went - it was the 'Big City' that I enjoyed; it reminded me of a much larger New Orleans. You can't imagine how short 48 hours is, but if you played your cards right and got on the train the evening before your pass began you could manage to stay in London for two nights. London

IT'S DANGEROUS TO FLAG
A BUS WITH YOUR TORCH

The perils of travel in London, particularly during the wartime blackout, led to death and injury among the British population. For Americans, unused to the traffic system, it brought home the additional dangers faced by those fighting on the Home Front. This poster, produced by the London Transport Office, warned against the use of a torch, waved in the face of a bus driver.

London's stations were drab places in wartime, often neglected, overworked and grimy. Paddington, seen here in 1942, was no exception.

was only about an hour from Whittlesford and we got off the train at the Liverpool Street Station where trains were arriving or departing constantly. I can never remember a station like Liverpool Street that was not damp and clammy and the concrete platform hard underfoot.

I did not tarry on the platform once I had found my way, but hurried to leave the place. Probably, like everyone else, I had a destination in mind. But when I got a chance I slipped into a seedy little teashop attached to the Station for a cup of tea and a not too sweet roll, all for less than a silver six pence - twelve cents, American. You could get other dishes there, but pubs had taught me that there were English standbys on the menu that I didn't like. I just wasn't up to kidney pie, Welsh rarebit, blood sausage and a few other hearty English dishes, but then what would and Englishman have thought about grits, hamburgers or hot dogs, things I was familiar with? Fish and chips could be had nearby in a shop and this, too, took some getting used to. I knew that my selection was limited, so I stuck to what I knew.

I found a seat and when the waitress asked, *"Wha'kin oi do f'ye maite"*? I answered, "Tea and sweet roll, please." I watched as the she brewed my tea; scalding hot water spewed into a teapot from a gleaming copper faucet that at one time had been chrome plated. In a rush, the waitress slid the teapot, a heavy chinaware mug, sugar cubes - precious sugar - a small bowl, a cream pitcher and a sweet roll on my clean, but worn table. For some reason English tea made and

Evacuees crowd a London railway platform early in the war destined for the comparative safety of the countryside. Later, many mothers were tempted to bring their children home to the cities, despite dire warnings.

served in England seems to taste better than tea made anywhere else. I don't know why, but it always has been and still is. Even tea that I have bought in London and brought home to the States never tastes the same here as it does in England. The door from the teashop opened out onto a wide cobblestone street where a bevy of Americans and every other nationality, were trying to catch the rare taxi, a bus or go to the underground. I always took a taxi, as I had not mastered the underground and buses were far too complicated. I didn't learn how to use the underground until more than 34 years later; buses are still a riddle.

The London taxi of WWII was a story all by itself. Vaguely, it reminded me of a hybrid cross between a stagecoach and an automobile. The passengers rode in a comfortable large rounded coach, Victorian, with soft but slick leather seats and grand doors that slide open on either side. In the rear there was a small window; up front a large plate glass window separating passengers from the driver, who was only partially protected from the elements. The hood seemed impossibly small and the small engine sounded like that of a Model 'T' Ford. Whoever designed them must have had the narrow London streets in mind; they could turn in their own length. Shades of Henry Ford, you could choose any colour you wanted so long as it was black and the brass was always brightly polished. One could never mistake them for passenger cars.

The entrance to The Strand tube station.

A poignant wartime scene on a station platform in London, as a young wife waves goodbye to her soldier husband.

26

London taxi drivers like those in big cities the world over, were not above taking advantage of a young 'Yank'. It happened to me on my first trip to the Big 'L'. I hailed a taxi driver and told him to take me to a certain address. I got in the cab and rode for several miles before he stopped and said, 'This is it, guv'ner.' I stepped out, paid him the princely sum of ten 'bob' - about two dollars - for the ride, tipped him one shilling and thanked him. After he drove off, I looked around and discovered much to my chagrin that I was only one block from where he had picked me up; so much for youth and ignorance.

After finishing my snack in the tea-room I took my bag and stepped out onto the dark grey cobblestone street fronting the station where I hailed a taxi. It was a good long way to Regent Street where the Reindeer Officers Club was located, but the trip was always interesting, for the driver frequently passed by St. Paul's Cathedral. Surprisingly, we passed little evidence of bomb damage on the way.

British Intelligence was clever and managed to tease German Intelligence - something we didn't seem to do too well. They capitalized on the reality that large areas of London had little or no bomb damage. When German aircrew, especially pilots, were shot down on their raids over London they were driven through the city on a very long circuitous route, never passing a single bomb damaged area. The story goes that the captured aircrews were astounded. British intelligence knew the PoWs would write home about their trip through London and the lack of damage they saw.

Regent Street is a long curving street with wide sidewalks lined by a nearly continuous facade of imposing low buildings and a short walk brings you to Piccadilly Circus. It is not only a hub in London, but also the location of a famous bronze statue of Eros, which I did not get to see because it was boarded-up and sandbagged to protect it from bombs. (During the spring of 1977 my wife Allison and I were in London and I thought, 'Aha, I'll get to see Eros' and that is where we headed at the first opportunity. Guess what - Eros was boarded up again to protect it from the football fans. I did not get to see Eros until 1992). The dark stone arches on Regent Street at Piccadilly were famous to servicemen for something else. The chances were that if you walked under those arches, a lady of the night would sidle up to you darkness and in a stage whisper, say, "Condoms, Mister, condoms, Mister." For boys, just become men - or so they thought - what a kick!

The Reindeer Club, one of those buildings in Regent Street, had a reception desk and a large reading room whose reading racks were full of current papers and magazines. English lady volunteers staffed the club and managed the desk to assign Officers quarters for their visit to London. I received my biggest surprises from one of the lady hostesses on my first trip in London in the late fall of 1943. The taxi let me out and I picked up my bag and climbed the steps up to the entrance. Double doors opened into a big open reception room with comfortable chairs situated about the room. On one side there was a reception desk and on the other a rack of newspapers. The only people in the large room were two ladies behind the receptionist's desk. Slightly uncomfortable, not sure whether I wanted to stay there, I decided to sit down and read a paper and collect my wits before signing for a room. So I walked over to the paper rack,

Rows of London taxi cabs vie with other traffic on a busy day.

took up the London *Times*, sat down and began to read. Not long afterward I noticed one of the ladies, who had been at the desk, walking toward me. I was struck by her poise, as she was a handsome, obviously genteel lady; her hair was brunette with a few silver streaks and she was well dressed. I put the paper down and stood up as she approached. With a friendly, but inquisitive, twinkle in her eye she asked me if my name was Russell. Puzzled, I told her that it was and asked who told her. She replied, "No one, you just look like a Russell." I could not believe what I was hearing and was sure that someone was pulling my leg, so I looked around; no one else was in the room but her and her colleague and me. She was sincere. We had a long conversation and I discovered that her married name had been Russell and that she had two or three sons all of whom were officers in the Royal Navy. Afterwards I would make it a point to invite her to dinner when I was in London. Through her I met some incredibly interesting people, including Guy Gibson who led the attack on and destroyed dams in the Ruhr valley for which he had been awarded the Victoria Cross. Also, she arranged for me to date a Russian Princess, Irena Obelinski, who was an acquaintance of hers. Irena was a pretty girl but big and almost raw-boned, whose family had fled Russia after the Revolution. In no way did she fit my concept of a real princess; she was just an ordinary girl, or so I thought. We and another couple toured the nightspots of London, at least those that were open. I had only one date with her. But there were many other things to find out about London, sometimes just as surprising.

Rooms were not always available, as the Reindeer Club did not make reservations. In that case, if they were full up the hostesses would locate one for us. In early 1944 the room they found us for two nights was directly over a railroad track and every time a train rumbled under us the sound woke us up. After that episode I began to look for more commodious quarters and found that two or three of us could rent a private apartment in a residential hotel - we would call it a condominium now - for not much more than it cost to stay at the Reindeer Club. The one we selected was located right off the Pall Mall (pronounced 'Pell Mell') in a posh, upper class neighbourhood only a few blocks from Buckingham Palace. The owner of the suite that we rented was away in the wars. It was a luxury apartment where meals were served *en suite* and I lodged there whenever I had a 48-hour pass in London.

Frequently, I would go to London with friends and we would sight see during the day. Even in the middle of the war, there were good restaurants, bars in the hotels, pubs, shops, the theatre and many historic places to see. Ernest Lang, Macie Marlowe and I discovered one of my all time favourite Chinese restaurants overlooking Piccadilly Circus. Fortunately, Lang was older than we were and obviously well educated and it was him who suggested that we see Samuel Johnson's London and many other historic places. Lang, like Marlowe, was married. As for me, I was footloose and fancy free, ready to bring on the girls - Hallelujah! Later, I found my own way about London.

Food was rationed and the problem was: how do you ration food in a restaurant? The British solved it by decreeing that you could not spend more then ten 'bob' in a restaurant. If you were hungry you could go to more than one restaurant, but that was anything but patriotic.

'Lang, Marlowe and I found a way to have a substantial dinner - the Chinese restaurant that

Life went on despite the war.

Feeding 45 Millions -
MARKETS

On the other side of the Atlantic stories and pictures of the London Blitz persuaded many otherwise neutral observers that the Nazi terror had gone far enough. But US servicemen, seeing the damage for themselves, were shocked by what they saw. On the left, a dramatic poster emphasising the importance of London's markets. Below, the reality. A milkman delivers pints in a wrecked London street.

I just mentioned; we would each order a ten bob dish and share with one another. It was not only superb food, but it satisfied our appetites as well as our stomachs: our favourites were chicken chow mien with crispy noodles, chop suey, egg foo yung and shrimp fried rice with Chinese tea, all for less than £1 10 shillings. I never failed to go to that Chinese restaurant and when Allison and I were in London in 1977 we went to the same restaurant in the same place above Piccadilly and found the food was still good, but not the same.

The theatre district operated through the war to help keep up morale and there were some excellent shows. For one, I saw 'Strike a New Note' at the Prince of Wales Theatre on Coventry

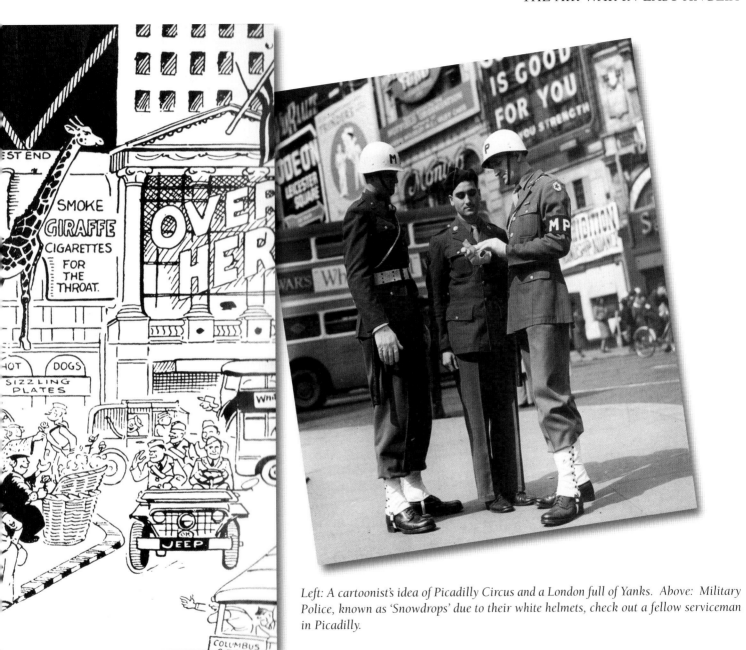

Left: A cartoonist's idea of Picadilly Circus and a London full of Yanks. Above: Military Police, known as 'Snowdrops' due to their white helmets, check out a fellow serviceman in Picadilly.

Overpaid, oversexed and over here. So the saying went. But the presence of the Americans was a huge boost to British morale. Here US airmen feed pigeons in Trafalgar Square.

St. The 'Programme' noted that, "If an Air Raid Warning be received during the performance the audience will be informed. The warning will not necessarily mean that a raid will take place. Those desiring to leave the Theatre may do so, but the performance will continue." How about that for a stiff upper lip?

There wasn't much to buy in wartime London. Clothes, shoes, food and you name it were rationed; the price tag wasn't too high, but without Ration coupons it might as well have been a million dollars. The only coupons that I ever got were for a pair of shoes. We could buy books, jewellery, antique, etc. without coupons, but so what. In Jermyn Street I did purchase a spectacular carved Meerschaum pipe with an amber stem for about £15 and a very small and ancient water colour of 1600s' sailing ships in the English Channel for about the same price from an art gallery. For the most part we wandered around in London, sightseeing during the day and pub-crawling; at night my fancy turned to girls. They were scarcer than you would think, but there were enough.

It is hard to imagine how short a 'forty-eight hour pass' can be when you're having fun. Always I left London heading for 'home' planning the next trip.

Although I heard many Air Raid alarms in London, only once did I hear bombs fall during an air raid. However, during a balmy and sunny June day in 1944, about a month after the invasion, I was in Oxford Street near Hyde Park when the sirens began to wail. It was in broad daylight and that was unusual. All the Londoners' ran for the Air Raid Shelters but I began to look skyward searching for German bombers. For a few minutes I heard nothing but sirens and then I began to hear anti-aircraft batteries open up to the south where I saw greasy bursts of flak appear several thousand feet in the sky. As the flak got closer, judgement whispered 'get in the Air Raid Shelter' but curiosity prompted me to continue looking for the cause of the commotion. Suddenly, there appeared amidst the flak bursts a small, stubby-winged, flying object with no propeller and a cylinder that resembled a smoke pipe on top the fuselage. It was going like a 'bat out of hell' and was making a noisy popping racket much like a 'raspberry' - what in the world? My eyes followed it across London and on the north side of the city, the motor stopped and it plunged downward. For seconds all was quiet except for the sirens and then there was a loud muffled explosion. Next day's newspapers announced that Hitler's vengeance weapons, the V-1 bombs had arrived. We had been wondering why all the bombing of apparently empty spaces along the beaches of France - now we had our answer.'

Forty-eight hour pass to London, winter 1944
by Ernest E. 'Ernie' Russell, adapted from A Mississippi Fighter Pilot in WWII

St Paul's Cathedral in the Blitz.

DOODLEBUGS

'After our first few passes the Germans decided that there was too much debauchery going on in London. The serious-minded Krauts sent the Buzz Bombs to stem the tide. The British referred to them as 'infernal nuisances'. Masters of understatement – I thought that anything that could pulverise a city block in the twinkling of an eye was something more than a nuisance…right here I am able to recall a scene that delineates the indomitable British spirit. One afternoon I saw a nice little old gentleman with bowler hat, pince-nez and umbrella. We were both strolling along in the park when one of the 'nuisances' came over with its Maytag engine popping loudly. All of a sudden the engine cut out – time to take cover! I dived to earth behind a great elm tree. Not my milquetoast friend – he stood his ground right out in the open. There was a dreadful explosion a few blocks away. The old gentleman drolly exclaimed, 'By God, that bugger was close!' He then continued on with his leisurely stroll, swinging his umbrella, while I stood there flabbergasted and visibly shaken.'

Ben Smith Jr., Chick's Crew.

WRENS, WAAFS AND FANYS

'We always rode the train to London when our crew got a forty-eight hour pass. It was about a two-hour ride and a glorious experience. The trains in England were standard size and they

Women on both sides of the Atlantic played a vital role both on the Home Front and in supporting the military. The poster above reminds women working in factories of the need for safety over fashion, while the ATS poster exhorts women to join the Auxiliary Territorial Service.

literally *flew*. Some of the cars had the configuration of American cars, but some were the antique carriage cars with doors leading from compartments directly outside. These trains were literally loaded to the gunwales with humanity, most of them young and in the armed forces. After the Yanks came to England, few civilians cared or dared to ride the British trains, not that there was any danger but rather because they were so noisy and riotous. As soon as we were on and the doors slammed shut, the engineer gave a ridiculous little beep with his whistle, and within seconds we were rocking along at break-neck speed. A liberal sprinkling of females, WRNS, WAAFs and ATS were always on board, as were British soldiers and sailors returning from leave from Scotland, the North Country, and the Midlands. The British girls were a bit more reserved than we. The icebreaker was to offer them an American cigarette, which they never refused, saying something that sounded like, "Thanks veddy much." In turn they would offer us a 'Players', one of their brands, but there were no takers. In a short time everyone in the car had made friends, and we were soon shouting and laughing. Miraculously a bottle would appear and would be passed up and down the car. After a time we would be singing to the tops of our voices with our British friends and before we got to London we had gotten somewhat lugubrious, embracing and making many sentimental declarations of love and kinship.

The train always came into the same station, St. Pancras. It was an enormous hangar-like structure with the entire roof ribbed and covered with glass skylighting. The huge station was a vortex of eddying humanity as hissing clouds of escaping steam and whistles blowing insanely sped the great throngs on their way. The loud speakers, sounding extra-terrestrial, were never silent. Refreshment stands run by the Red Cross and NAAFI were crowded with young servicemen, frantically grabbing a cold sands and cup of hot tea before boarding. Always there was a British regiment in full battle kit embarking for the shooting war with wives and girl friends hanging on to the last possible moment, then weeping piteously as men-folk shouted words of encouragement. And all about was that definitive sound of war, the tread of hobnail boots…'

London Revisited, Ben Smith Jr, Chick's Crew

Days of steam.

NORWICH TO LONDON

'Our crew received a 72-hour pass to London and Virgil, Pete, Shorty and I caught the train out of Norwich to London, about a four-hour trip because of the numerous stops made along the way. The coaches, considerably smaller than those in the US, consisted of individual compartments with seats facing each other and doors opening directly onto the loading platform. In other words, there was no aisle going the length of the coach and no way to go from one compartment to the adjoining one - also, no access to a rest room!'

Staff Sergeant Dale R. VanBlair

FOGGY LONDON TOWN

'It was November 1943 and a very foggy night. The occasion was one of my first visits to London and we were returning on the train. The word 'Bovril' appeared at one of the stations. Nothing else was on the sign. Another GI said to me "It's a bad fog, really bad, he's going round in a circle. We've been through Bovril twice before!" We did not know, being foreigners, that Bovril was a drink!

Jim Johnson

A statue of Thomas Paine stands in his birthplace at Thetford. He was to become one of America's great historical figures, championing independence and publishing his anti-loyalist monograph, Common Sense in 1776. His book Rights of Man helped usher in the Age of Enlightenment.

ENGLISH RAILROADS

'One of the things I liked was railroad trains. I liked the English railroads. They were just real neat. The cars ran smooth; they were fast; everything worked good. Seemed like better than ours. But the only chance that I got to ride a train was when we went to London.'

Sergeant Robert 'Bob' S. Cox, mechanic, 466th Bomb Group

PASTORAL VISIONS

'The train rides from Thetford to London enabled us to view the quaint beauty of the small towns and rural countryside of England. The deep-green hedgerows, rolling fields and slow-flowing streams of East Anglia were scenes out of 18th Century pastoral paintings. All too soon our two-day vacation from the war would come to an end. We would return to combat somewhat hung over, but dedicated to our rendezvous with our duty and our destiny.'

The Year I Can't Forget, James E. O'Connor, co-pilot, *La-Dee-Doo* crew, 388th Bomb Group 10 July 1944

Thetford today.

HOME FROM HOME

LAVENHAM

'I didn't spend much time in Lavenham. Our off duty hours were spent at the base, or, if we had a three day pass, we would go to London. Lavenham was a typical, quaint old English village. It was just a small place with a "White Swan" pub, a few merchants, an old stone church and many of the homes had thatched roofs. The church is a beautiful old stone building with its tall bell tower dating back to the 1600s. I attended services there one Sunday and felt welcome by the congregation. The permanent party personnel looked upon the village as 'theirs'. After all, they had been there a long time before we arrived and we were just passing through.'

Dean M. Bloyd

RAF and American airmen's signatures in the Swan Inn at Lavenham, Suffolk. Plaques in the square, church and the Swan Inn, (now a hotel) commemorate the airfield nearby.

St Peter and St Paul church, Lavenham.

16TH APRIL 1945

'It took me several days to regain the knack of riding a bicycle with complete confidence, for I had not ridden one for twenty years. My first trip was a short one, to Lavenham Church, whose tower was visible from the station and whose bells might be heard across the fields. Lavenham Church is one of the glories of Suffolk and ranks as one of the half-dozen or so very best churches in that county, which above all others in churches of the thirteenth, fourteenth and fifteenth centuries. The Black Death, in the middle of the fourteenth century, halved the population of the county, but the building of churches continued practically unabated. Spirit of local pride led the people of Lavenham to build a church bigger and more splendid than the one the people of Long Melford were working on.'

Suffolk Summer, **John T. Appleby.**

'Over a period of eight months in 1945 38-year old John T. Appleby, an American from Arkansas who was stationed in Suffolk, travelled the length and breadth of East Anglia and beyond exploring churches and collecting brass rubbings. He travelled by rail but mostly on his faithful old cycle 'The

Squadron insignia at Lavenham in August 1972. (Steve Gotts)

THE AIR WAR IN EAST ANGLIA

*Green Hornet' with its out-sized pre-war 'balloon' tyre, already worn smooth, and which could not be replaced. The Green Hornet served him faithfully for two and a half months during which time at a conservative estimate, he covered over 2,000 miles. Appleby's book, Suffolk Summer was privately published in 1948. (In Bury St Edmunds the Old English Rose Garden in the Abbey grounds pays homage to those lost in service with the 94*th* Bomb Group in WW2. At the entrance is a plaque reading: 'The construction of this old English rose garden is due to the generosity of an American friend of this borough Mr. John Appleby, who was stationed near Bury St. Edmunds during the war whilst a member of the United States Eighth Air Force. Mr. Appleby became very attached to this old town and its historic associations and also to the surrounding countryside with its numerous pictur-esque villages and fine churches. His regard and affection for this portion of England and its people is portrayed in his book 'Suffolk Summer' written after his return to the United States. The Royalties from the sales of this book have been generously given to the Borough for making and effecting improvements to this Rose Garden.)'*

IPSWICH GIRLS

'When you see a girl in khaki or air force blue with a bit of ribbon on her tunic - remember she didn't get it for knitting more socks than anyone else in Ipswich.'
A Short Guide to Great Britain **(which was issued to every GI)**

NIGHTS OUT IN IPSWICH

'Perhaps it was just a coincidence, perhaps it was a touch of clairvoyance but the only book I brought with me from America -a book hastily purchased in New York City for shipboard reading - was Dickens's *Pickwick Papers*. I had space in my duffle for just one book; I wanted one that was amusing, lengthy and yet compact and concerned with England, which my hunch told me was our destination... It was a happy choice, for I found myself lying in the cramped stateroom or on the crowded deck rediscovering half-forgotten treasures in the adventures of Pickwick and his company in London, Bath, Bury St. Edmunds and Ipswich. It was even more apropos, I decided a week after our arrival in England, when I found myself walking down the streets of that same Ipswich and stopping at a hotel for a beer - a hotel named the Great White Horse - the very same hotel, I recalled with delight, where transpired that epic incident of the Lady with the Yellow Curl Papers.

No city could have been farther removed from that Dickensian world than Ipswich in the autumn and winter of 1942. Dirty, crowded, noisy, evil smelling, it was then a composite of the smaller English provincial metropolis at war. Though it retained to some degree its basic East Anglian character, it was now in addition a roaring industrial town, a busy port and an amuse-ment centre for troops of a dozen Allied nations.... It was a dirty, smelly, crowded old town after dark, this Ipswich of the war. Little streams of urine ran down from doorways into the gutter and in some doorways there were the dark forms of a boy and a girl pressed close together. The

"My goodness, my Guinness"

Above: A wartime advertisement for Guinness stout, with the local gent being pursued into the pub by hordes of thirsty American GIs.

Right: The Cricketers pub, Ipswich, popular with American airmen in the 1940s.

night air had a musty, old, stale smell; the smell of fried fish, of coal smoke, of horse manure and of fog and the sea. It smelled of beer and rain and aged, mouldy stones. The flat-paned windows were gaping and vacant, the streets narrow, cobble-stoned and dark. It was not until midnight that they became silent and empty and you could hear again the echo of your own footsteps and far down by the River Orwell the clanking and screaming of the trains.

Our first stop was the YMCA where we could shave and wash in that greatest of luxuries - hot water. Then we went upstairs and had breakfast for a few pennies. Coffee and hot buttered toast, with jam and a few pleasant words from the girl in slacks who worked behind the counter… If we had errands we would attend to them. The dry cleaners usually, for we always had a load of filthy clothes. Vera at the shop…could do the impossible and rush our most urgent orders through in not the usual ten days but in two - or if we spoke nicely - perhaps even one! And there was always the beautiful girl walking up the hill to work - who always smiled and waved to us.

There were all types of public houses in Ipswich. The most popular of these were the ones where girls congregated - 'The Cricketers', 'The Great White Horse', 'The Mulberry Tree' and these were usually bedlams of sound and excitement while the beer lasted. There were the more sedate places like 'The Crown and Anchor' and 'The Golden Lion' and 'The Unicorn' where the

The Plough in Ipswich today.

American would occasionally enjoy a quiet hour in less frantic surroundings. There were the less-imposing pubs like 'The Fox', 'The Plough', 'The Blue Coat Boy' and 'The Waggon and Horses' where there was less formality and which were "Off Limits" to our troops at various times. There were others - family pubs, workers' pubs, railway pubs, seaport pubs, large and small ones, clean and dirty ones; with names like 'The Queen's Arms' and 'The Welcome Sailor', 'The Running Buck' and 'The Spotted Cow', 'The Griffin' and 'The Saracen's Head' and we explored most of them. As we grew to know Ipswich each of us had his favourites where he knew the barkeeps, the regular customers and the local traditions.

Perhaps the chief attraction of Ipswich was the girls. It seemed to us then a town of girls, with a high proportion of young and pretty ones and their behaviour was nothing like that of girls we had known at home. In the evening they walked along the pavements in pairs, smiling, swinging their supple hips in short skirts, looking after the soldiers, whispering "Hi, Yank!" or whistling a phase from "*Yankee Doodle.*" Many were young - fourteen, fifteen or sixteen, though we could not judge how old they were and they always said they were eighteen at least. They had beautiful flowing hair, they wore tight sweaters and flat-heeled shoes and they spoke that sing-song Suffolk dialect that often we could not fathom. They went unescorted to the dance halls and to the public houses and it was there that we met them.

At the sign of the White Horse.

The Regent Cinema, Ipswich, as it looks today. Opened in 1929 it would have been one of the town's most popular venues during the war.

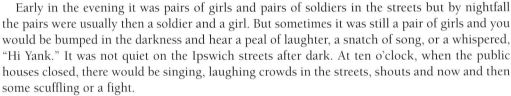

Early in the evening it was pairs of girls and pairs of soldiers in the streets but by nightfall the pairs were usually then a soldier and a girl. But sometimes it was still a pair of girls and you would be bumped in the darkness and hear a peal of laughter, a snatch of song, or a whispered, "Hi Yank." It was not quiet on the Ipswich streets after dark. At ten o'clock, when the public houses closed, there would be singing, laughing crowds in the streets, shouts and now and then some scuffling or a fight.

There was a dance at Ipswich almost every night in the week, either at the Co-operative Hall or St. Lawrence's Church Hall. At both these hall's soldiers came in groups and the girls came unescorted and paid their own way, which resulted in a somewhat variegated choice of partners, ranging from pretty children of not more than fourteen to middle-aged spinsters and offering an equally wide range of dancing styles.

The trucks left the parking lot in Princes Street at eleven and here were soldiers and girls saying good night and other soldiers loudly calling the names of their friends, trying to locate their own company truck. Occasionally a belly-full of bitter played tricks and a soldier would awaken the next morning in a strange bed at the wrong aerodrome and sometimes not at an aerodrome at all but in an even more unfamiliar bed at the Ipswich Police Station.

The truck ride home was an ordeal; the same thirty men were on board but it was eleven o'clock now and not seven and there was shouting and laughter and singing and loud, violent

Film poster from 1943 advertising 'The Gentle Sex', made to help promote the work of women in the armed services: 'A Tribute to the Glorious Womanhood of Britain.'

The Swan, Ipswich, as it looks today.

arguments about nothing and occasionally a scuffle and always a few men asleep. The truck roared though the silent villages of Suffolk, leaving a bellowed wake of "Bell-bottomed Trousers," or "God Bless America" - and the persistent monologue of one raucous soldier, describing to a disinterested world the details of a probably imaginary doorway romance.

There was nothing restful in these nights in town; there was little relaxation; there was little inspirational and nothing of beauty. They served merely for an escape, a blowing off of steam, a release from confinement and they were the only diversion that the world could offer us at the time.

Many of us and certainly many people of Ipswich were disturbed by what they saw and heard and by the easy familiarity of the young girls that roamed the streets and frequented the public houses. We had many a long and serious discussion on this topic in Hut Seven but we never came to any conclusions. Was it wartime excitement and the ever-present threat of death from the sky that had induced this "gather ye rosebuds" attitude? Was it a relaxation of parental influence caused by the absence of fathers, by working mothers and the lack of family life? Was it the sudden presence of a crowd of strange and carefree men in uniform? Or was it all these things that, summed up, were the impact of war on this town and inevitably brought with it new and lowered, standards?

Ipswich from the air.

Was it happening in other towns in England and in other countries in war? Was it happening at home, in our own land, in our own hometown?

We hoped that it wasn't but we feared in our hearts that it was.'

Here We Are Together, The Notebook of an American Soldier in Britain, Robert S. Arbib Jr.

'HEY THERE LIMEY...'

'I was born in London but at the height of the war my family moved to the coastal town of Ipswich in Suffolk. It was there that I gained my first impression of real live Americans. When the first Americans reached our town, it did not take most of them long to find our number one landmark, the English pub.

I will never forget the first American soldiers I saw. There were about five of them who were very much under the influence of alcohol. Their hats were on the backs of their heads and their ties were every way but the right way. Two of them were sitting on the kerb and the others were holding up a lamp post. They were singing. My immediate thought was, "If this is a sample of

How they got the war news. Locals listen to the wireless in the bar of a Suffolk pub.

the American who have come over to help us, heaven help us". In the next few weeks the town literally became full of American soldiers. My first encounter with these GIs left the impression with me that they were loud showoffs. They would call, "Hey there Limey," after the girls as they walked down the streets. This used to embarrass us English girls to death.'

WARTIME WEDDING

The wedding of Clarence "Red" Burnett from Chillicot, Illinois and Lillian Lambert was on 20 May 1945 in St. Clements Episcopal Church in Ipswich

'Got married in October 1944 and we had a room in my wife's sister's house in Sproughton Road, Ipswich. Providing I was in by 7 o'clock in the morning I was allowed to spend the night off base. It was about 10 miles from the Hitcham depot to where my wife lived and for the rest of my time in England I cycled there after coming off duty and back each morning. The trip took about an hour and in the cold and the blackout it wasn't easy.'

Marion Smith of the 4th Strategic Air Depot

Bury St Edmunds from the air, as it looks today.

BURY ST EDMUNDS

'Places that I grew to frequent with my English soldier friends were the Athenaeum, the Salvation Army Canteen in Abbeygate Street, where one could get a cup of tea and a sandwich at any hour of the day, and the YMCA Hostel where one could have tea in the garden, overlooking the gentle valley to the south and the hill rising beyond it.

The Athenaeum Canteen was a unique contribution of the people of Bury St. Edmunds to the entertainment of the troops stationed there. In peacetime Bury is a garrison town, the headquarters of the Suffolk Regiment. In wartime, Blenheim Camp was enlarged and made an Infantry Training Centre. Consequently the streets were thronged with fresh-faced recruits, still awkward in their unfamiliar uniforms, as well as with members of the Royal Air Force and the Eighth Air Force, who had many fields in the vicinity.

The Athenaeum Club formed the south side of Angel Hill, the large square before the Abbey Gate. On the ground floor of the Club was a large and gracious Eighteenth Century Assembly Room, used for subscription dances, lectures and the like in peacetime. A group of townspeople, headed by the Mayor, Mr. E. L. D. Lake, convened the room into a canteen for the troops. Committees of volunteers manned the refreshment counter where one could get tea, sand-

AND PLEASE
DON'T THROW
FOOD
AWAY EITHER

wiches and cakes and a lending library and a mending service occupied each corner of the room. The fare provided by the "Athenium", as it came to be called was recognized as the best in Bury and it was so cheap that no one could eat a whole shillings-worth, no matter how hungry he was. One afternoon Pte Bernard West, a lad with a healthy appetite, and I, as an experiment, ate the largest tea we could possibly hold, and at the bitter end we found that we had spent only one-and-six between us.

When the Athenaeum Canteen was closed at the end of September 1945, it was computed that almost a million and a half servicemen and women had entered its doors. When that figure is translated into tea and sandwiches, and then into the cutting of bread, the spreading of jam, and the washing of cups, one can form an idea of the work of these noble women.'

Suffolk Summer, **John T. Appleby**

TREATS

'I remember well the airfields, the busy streets, the dances, the bomber jackets and especially the indescribable treats often bestowed on us by the Yanks: chocolate, which in luxury-starved

For most American servicemen the conditions under which the British had survived since the outbreak of war came as a shock. While the United States remained untouched by the direct effects of the war, in Britain shortages of food and other essential resources meant the enforcement of rationing, begun in October 1939. Above left: a poster exhorts military personnel note to throw food away. Above tight: A ration card entitled the owner to three pints of milk a week.

American servicemen, with their healthy looks and smart uniforms and their access to many luxuries denied to the home population, proved a popular attraction!

All too often, wartime meals ended up as 'pitiful travesties'.

Britain was but a faint memory; oranges; Ipana toothpaste; and scented soaps. But having escaped from our homes on the continent, my friends and I had few illusions about what would happen if the Germans succeeded in invading England; and we instinctively knew that the presence of the Eighth Air Force meant more to us than having dancing partners and chocolate treats.

At night the Eighth Air Force boys would drift into Bury St. Edmunds where weekly dances were held at the Corn Exchange building. This venerable building had, no doubt, never seen such an outpouring of energy. How those Yanks could dance! The walls shook as couples jitterbugged wildly to the popular tunes of the time: *"Don't sit under the Apple Tree," "In The Mood," "Give Me One Minute More," "Chattanooga Choo-Choo"* and many others. They did this at night, while during the day they were making history, fighting and dying in the greatest war of all time.

At Bury St. Edmunds we encountered very few American servicewomen - WACs, nurses, etc but on visits to London or Edinburgh we met them on the subway, in the streets, or while staying at the service clubs. To us, they were the epitome of smartness and glamour. Their uniforms were cut of fine, dark cloth, compared to our own thick and rough khakis. The names of the towns they came from reminded us of our geography lessons in secondary school in Vienna - Tuscaloosa, Phoenix and San Francisco. And, like their male counterparts, they spoke with accents right out of the John Wayne movies we loved. We also liked Dick Haymes, Betty Grable and *Gone With The Wind*; in fact, almost any movie or movie star.'

Frances Nunnally

DEPRESSING FOOD

'In Bury St. Edmunds I went to the Angel, where Mr. Pickwick and Sam Weller stayed and in whose courtyard Sam had his head doused with cold water; is in Angel Hill, directly across from the Abbey Gate. It is in the best tradition of the old English inns and even in wartime the hostess, Mrs. Robertson, contrived to keep enough of the amenities that one always entered its door with a warm glow of anticipation and the assurance of a cheery welcome. The meals were pitiful travesties, and from the kitchen, which once boasted of its roast beef there issued now jugged hare, skimpy bits of roast chicken, and morsels of boiled fish. Wartime dinners, as decreed by the Ministry of Food consisted of soup, made usually from a powder; meat or fish minute portions, two vegetables, usually boiled potatoes and greens, and a sweet made with a minimum of sweetening, at maximum price of five shillings. These meals were depressing even under the best of conditions and I never ceased to marvel that the English, traditionally heavy eaters, especially of meat (of which they were now limited to 22 ounces a week), could bear up under them for six long and weary years without open rebellion. Their endurance of bombings, V-1s and V-2s was heroic and inspiring, but it took a different, and no less heroic and though less inspiring, sort of courage to face this dull, stodgy, deadening, flat, and uninspiring food day after day. Every leaf of tea had to be counted, even grain of sugar hoarded and every bit of fat treasured and minute portions of meat won by patient endurance in an interminable queue. The

English people whom I knew accepted rationing very cheerfully and every one agreed that the Ministry of Food had done a good job in ensuring that every one got his fair share of the stocks available. Indeed, so effectively was this done that I often heard it asserted that the health of the nation as a whole had never been better. No one went hungry and everyone got his fair share, even though it was a fair share of such delicacies as potatoes and Spam.'

Suffolk Summer, **John T. Appleby**

BY CYCLE TO BECCLES

'On my map of Suffolk I had marked the locations of all the brasses in the county by underlining in red the places where they were to be found. The really notable ones, however, were shown by a big red circle. Three such circles dotted the map in the neighbourhood of Beccles, in the northeast corner of the county. On the 18th June I loaded my bicycle on the train and started for Beccles, which I planned to use as a base of operations.

Spam was perhaps the most well-known of the foodstuffs that Americans brought with them. For the British public, struggling to get to terms with life on rations, Spam was a tasty and welcome addition to their diet. Above right: Bottles of wine and spirits from wall art discovered at the old Aero Club at Bungay, Suffolk. (Flixton)

The Church of St Michael, Beccles. Note the tower, separate from the body of the church.

From Ipswich the train went north through quite new country to me, by way of Woodbridge, Saxmundham, and Halesworth. East Suffolk has some very pretty country, but it is flatter than the western part of the county and hence less interesting. I reached Beccles about noon and was fortunate enough to find a room at the 'King's Head Inn'. In the interval before lunch I had time to see the Perpendicular tower, which stands apart from the church, and the excellent carving in the south porch.

At the 'King's Head' that evening I had one of the best meals I had yet enjoyed in England. The main dish was a delicious great halibut steak, fresh from the sea, excellently grilled, and I arose from the table with an unaccustomed feeling of fullness about the middle.

East of the church the land drops down abruptly to the Beccles Marshes, through which winds the River Waveney. I sat on a bench at the edge of the churchyard and spent the evening looking out over the marshes and watching the mist rising from the river. It was an evening of perfect summer serenity, with the sunlight bathing the fields and trees with liquid gold.'

Suffolk Summer, **John T. Appleby**

FRAMLINGHAM

'About noon I started back for Bury St. Edmunds. Train schedules, involving a long wait at Ipswich, were not particularly satisfactory and it was such a perfect day that I decided to cycle back. My first stop was at Blythburgh, where there is one of the finest churches in Suffolk. It is

The castle at Framlingham

a vast building, towering above the marshes, with very fine stone carving, particularly around the south porch and a painted roof of great beauty. I went on to Framlingham, where there are the remains of the great castle where Mary Tudor rallied her followers after the death of Edward VI, when the succession appeared to be in doubt. All the interior buildings of the castle had been razed under the provisions of the will of an eccentric owner who directed that they be torn down to provide dwellings for the poor, and only the great outer walls remain. The church at Framlingham has the richly ornate tombs of the Mowbrays and the Howards, Dukes of Norfolk in succession to the turbulent Bigods.'

Suffolk Summer, John T. Appleby

Framlingham airfield was built in 1942 and was used by the United States Army Air Force Eighth Air Force. It later became an RAF station (Parham).

Eye airfield was constructed by the 827th and 859th US Army Engineer Battalions during 1943. It was completed early in 1944 and was assigned USAAF designation Station 138. Eye airfield was one of the last wartime airfields to be built in Britain. It was occupied by units of the 490th Bombardment Group, US 8th Air Force.

EYE TO EYE

'On the 14th, a very warm evening, I cycled to Occold, three miles south of Eye, and made a rubbing of the brass there, which is dated 1500. I stopped at Eye to visit the church but found it locked. Some of the best flush-work in East Anglia can be seen there. The tower is particularly fine, with the long, perpendicular, white lines of the flush-work accentuating the height. Usually flush-work is confined to ornamental, nonrepresentational patterns, but on the east end I found designs of the chalice and the ciborium and host in black flint, outlined with greyish-white stone. In the south porch is a curious variant of flush-work, with red brick taking the place of the flint. I stopped also at Brome Church, which has a round tower and curious mixture of arches in the interior, with round ones on the south and pointed ones on the north side of the interior.'

Suffolk Summer, John T. Appleby

CAMBRIDGE & BEYOND

WAR AND PEACE

'Cambridge is as comfortable a blend of war and peace as you could find anywhere in the United Kingdom, and all the side effects and currents of a world conflict can be seen and heard right from the time of arrival at the railway station. In one corner a large group of Italian prisoners in their maroon wool uniforms squat on their barracks bags and leather suitcases and smoke, whistle, or doze in the autumn sunlight. They are a cheerful, sun burnt, bored, well fed bunch, probably on their way to work on the farms of Norfolk. In the station restaurant American soldiers surround the counter eating meat pies and discussing the excellence of the coffee. The English are now turning out good coffee and this comes as one of the climaxes of the war as far as we are concerned.

Walking through the town you are made aware of the fact that this is a great center of university life until you reach the Red Cross Club on Trumpington Street. This is an ex-hotel right next to the smoke-gray battlements of King's College and the soldiers lounging in the doorway of the Red Cross, wondering what their next move is going to be, can look straight across at King's College Chapel and the clouds of pigeons wheeling outside the boarded-up stained glass windows. Along the streets the excellent book stores and print and liquor shops are filled with customers. Students flow and sweep along on either foot or bicycle in their blue and black gowns and long, trailing college scarves worn over turtle necked sweaters and tweed suits.

Down on the riverbank the Cam, choked with leaves, winds slowly along, encircles some of the colleges like a moat, and finally wanders off towards Grantchester under a bridge. Here there is a small, mild waterfall whose noise is sometimes lost in the sudden roar of a Marauder flying low and fast over the treetops.

The surface of the river is strewn with GIs in punts and canoes and the sight pleases the man who rents out the boats. For him the American Army has been an unqualified godsend in providing tourist trade that he never expected to see again after 1939.

Cambridge: an aerial view of King's College Chapel.

Signatures and squadron numbers smoked on the ceiling of the Airman's bar in the 'Eagle' in Benet Street, Cambridge.

"We really enjoy seeing you Yanks here now. Of course, some of you get drunk and lie around the market-place all night, but that's all right. It makes it seem like the old days again."

The rest of the people in Cambridge feel as he does and the only complaint that the college authorities have to make is that the average US Army visitor does not show the proper amount of curiosity about the place and does not make use of the free lectures and other sightseeing privileges.

This lack of curiosity might account for the fact there were so few GIs at the Town Meeting held in Cambridge on the night of October 8th. When the meeting broke up, a number of the audience went over to the Eagle Hotel across the street from the Exchange. Here, Ethel, the well-set brunette barmaid was setting them up right and left across the counter. She is one of the livelier institutions of Cambridge and her large public among the 8th Air Force all swear by her. Even on flying pay, aerial gunners and the like have a habit of going into a fiscal collapse when they least expect one, but Ethel has always tided her friends through such dark periods in their lives. What is more significant, she is always paid back.

On the wall of the Eagle Hotel's wash room among the usual frescoes and epigrams is pencilled this inscription: *"Never before in history have so many known so little about so much. Signed Benito Mussolini, Guard House, Italy."* This does not seem a bad motto either for an army educational program of a university town during wartime.'

A DAY AT CAMBRIDGE, John D. Preston,
Yank, the Army weekly magazine

ACADEMIA, AGRICULTURE AND AIRCRAFT

'Someone once said that the River Cam along the Cambridge "backs" was the most beautiful half-mile in England. Standing now on the carpet of green lawn of King's College on that bright June afternoon, I was in no mood to disagree. Here, if anywhere in England, was a spot where tradition, architecture, history and landscape blended into a perfect, harmonious whole. Here was the past in the magnificent old chapel and the perfect classic proportion of the adjacent Clare; here was age and beauty. Here, too, overhead was the present, as British bombers wheeled and manoeuvred in the afternoon sunlight. Here, too, was the future, walking about the court-yard in the uniform of air cadets - talking from window to window across the court - lazing idly at the riverbank. Here all ages met.

Cambridge University, if you excepted the sky above it, which invades all sanctuaries, was an island of peace and contemplation set in the stormy sea of war that swirled around Eastern England. The streets of the town were crowded with British airmen, WAAFs; farmers come to market, Americans who flocked to their club in the Bull Hotel. But once inside those massive iron gates, you left the noise and hurly-burly of the world outside; you entered a cloistered, ordered and somehow a remote world where every stone and every blade of grass cried out "I belong here…just here!"

Only the aeroplanes in the sky above seemed out of place. Rooks, yes, wheeling and turning above the tall trees across the river. But not Lancasters, Halifaxes, Wellingtons and Ansons. Could a man seriously ponder his Horace or his Newton with this new-celestial roar in his ears?

Cambridge: perfect surroundings for study and education.

The incongruity of war. A herd of sheep mingle with high explosive bombs destined for a squadron of Flying Fortresses in Cambridgeshire.

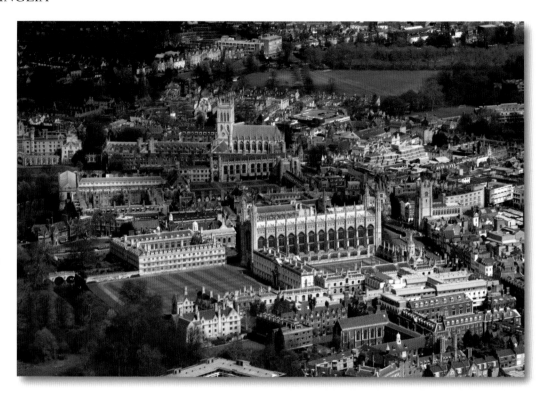

Present day aerial view of Cambridge and its colleges.

As I stood and thought, a voice behind me asked politely, "And what do you think of our college?"

I turned to see a thin, rather bent man in a shabby jacket and baggy trousers, with a three-day growth of beard, who was also admiring our surroundings and puffing damply on a pipe. "I think it's a beautiful place," I said. "I thought of coming here to study once - seven years ago. And so now I thought I'd like to come and see what I missed."

"And does it meet with your approval?"

"Unqualified," I said. "I can't imagine more perfect surroundings for study and for education. Although I suppose it was a bit more conducive to thought when those things were not over-head all the time."

"You get quite used to them, you know," he said, belching loudly by way of emphasis. "Of course, there's still a lot to be desired in the way of improvements but in some ways our system does give a man a sort of polish and if he exposes himself to it enough - a fairish education?'

'Our talk continued and led to American universities, which this disreputable looking character had once toured (and where, I thought, he probably had got his last haircut!) and to the various differences between American and English university life, to architecture and back to the Cambridge scene before us. "I suppose you'll want to go along the river to Granchester," he said, belching again with great unconcern. "Most Americans do. Rather a nice walk - Rupert Brooke, who lived in this college, made it quite sought after."

"I hadn't thought of that," I admitted. "I'd like to see the rooms -of some of the other Cambridge favourites though, Spenser and Herrick and Coleridge and even Milton.

"Quite. Yes, you'll doubtless enjoy seeing them, though there may be some young lads installed there now who have changed things around a bit. Well, getting late. Must be going. Glad to have seen you." And he was off.

Later that evening I asked Clement, my host, who this strange, unkempt, informal character could have been. I described him carefully, while Clement pondered a moment and then smiled… "Oh, that must have been old _____ he's a brilliant scholar really. One of the country's leading authorities on his subject. A bit eccentric but a good fellow. Knighted quite recently, as a matter of fact."

The next day Clement took me on a tour of the university. Though it was between terms and most of the students were gone, I enjoyed that walk around the university grounds and through the quiet courtyards. Here was the ancient Elizabethan brick of Queen's, here was old Trinity with its host of famous names, here was the dark, crumbled stone of Magdalene. …raftered dining halls with their carved oak tables black with age and their ancient nameless portraits on the wails. Here was a place for a young man to live and let history and knowledge and manners seep into his skin and run in his blood. Here while he studied he could see for himself the qualities that had slowly brought this gem to England and England its prominence in the world. He need not be taught English history here - it was all around him and if he listened he might still hear the whispered voices of Wordsworth and Newton, Darwin and Pitt, Cromwell and Milton and perhaps even Chaucer!

You couldn't help doing some thinking here at Cambridge - and that, I suppose, is just what it is for.'

Thoughts at Cambridge, Robert S. Arbib Jr.

'MAKING OUR OWN EXCITEMENT'

'Mostly, we had to make our own excitement. And that was in town. When I could, after supper, I would join the crowd going to see the sights of Cambridge to see the girls and to sample the wares at the Red Lion pub or various other public houses. Once in a blue moon, I would a chance to go town during the daytime to get a haircut, buy books, or just to gawk. I was intrigued by the handsome halls belonging to the colleges of the university and with the students and their flowing robes, but not enough to converse with any of them. We were in different leagues. Cambridge was beyond the radius of our bicycles, about eight miles, or, at least, that was our opinion, so we caught base transportation into town, which was another of the ubiquitous 'Six-bys' that served all base personnel. The 'bus' departed the base on schedule during the day and on most afternoons after supper and returned about eleven at night. An

The fact and the fantasy. An American airman walks out with a local girl in Suffolk (above), while the wall art from the airbase at Mendlesham (above right) shows a different point of view.

enlisted driver and a buddy generally rode in the cab; all the rest rode in the back. During the long summer days transportation departed and returned in broad daylight, but in the winter dark came early and it was pitch dark before we got home. The buses stopped for every GI, anywhere, often at all the small watering holes along the way. At each stop there was much jostling about to let people get on or off. Frequently, the first stop was a local pub just off the base at Duxford and another where we caught the train to London, Whittlesford.

At best it was 'airish' in the back, but then it was free. The truck was not sprung for comfort - that was not a priority - and the seats were inordinately hard, so when the driver hit a pothole or a curb it shivered your spine and bruised your posterior. Also, you might wind up on the bed of the truck when there was a sudden stop, which was not infrequent, because the narrow

As with most warm-blooded young men, the US servicemen dreamed of women. This piece of wall art was found at Shipdham.

Basic and uncomfortable, US trucks such as this 'Six-by' were familiar sights in and around the American bases and were popular methods of transport on Liberty Runs.

An Eastern Counties bus heads out to Yarmouth, typical of a scene in East Anglia during the 1940s. Such buses were real 'bone-shakers', and travelled miles at very slow speeds on rutted roads.

'Pubbing missions' were a popular GI pastime. The Mermaid, a short bicycle ride from Seething and Bungay airfields, was known colloquially as 'The Swinging Tits'.

8th Air Force crewman.

English roads were built for much smaller vehicular traffic and, at corners head on confrontations were not uncommon. Generally, it took less than a half-hour to reach the car parking lot in Cambridge. Once the truck pulled to a stop in the 'car park,' someone would drop the tailgate and we would depart in a mad scramble for our favorite haunts.

If I travelled into Cambridge during the day, it was to shop or get a haircut to escape the GI barber on base, but that was not guarantee. You had to watch the English barbers, also as they would cut your hair English style, that is long, and soon your locks would be around your ears - the Air Force frowned on long hair. There was little to buy in shops, and most of what was available was rationed; mainly, it was clothes and shoes, but you had to have coupons as they were rationed. There was no reason to buy food, except in restaurants where an individual was restricted to less than ten 'Bob' - ten shillings, about two dollars. Hardly any other items were available and these included antiques, most everything else was considered a luxury and had a wartime luxury tax of hundred per cent. As a result, antique silver and gold and books etc,

The desperate perils of fighting brought young men close, and the ever-present threat of death resulted in a devil-may-care attitude when off duty. Here the crew of "Round Trip Ticket' pose in front of their aircraft at Great Ashfield, Suffolk.

could be purchased for a pittance. Unfortunately, I was too young to have antiques on my mind.

Cambridge was a great place to 'pub-crawl' in, as it was a college town. Since I saw my first pub at Atcham they fascinated me. Every village in East Anglia had at least one and the larger towns, multiple public houses. Many pubs had been there for generations, and had become local institutions. The older pubs were from another era when the average person wasn't too tall, so most had low ceilings often supported by heavy, ancient, hand-hewn beams. The walls might be covered with antique red velvet or plush, but more often they were panelled with wood darkened by age and smoke. Sturdy tables and chairs filled the floor, and the bartender stood behind the bar pulling the "bowling pin" shaped levers to fill the pints. Unlike many of the bars etc in this country, most were spotlessly clean and the brass gleamed in the low light. Invariably, the light was dim and when you stepped inside, it would take a while for your eyes to adjust to it and the smoke; electric lighting had replaced candles and oil lamps not too many years ago. In villages on cold winter afternoon's logs would be burning in the fireplace; it was a most cozy place to be. Dartboards were ubiquitous.

It took a while to feel comfortable in the pubs as the English were very reserved and seldom spoke to strangers before being spoken to. This was especially true in the countryside, where ruddy-faced farmers and locals typically were distant and seldom raised their voices, but once you had broken their reserve, they were very friendly and took to us 'Yanks'. They did not take friendship lightly and countless lonesome GI's were invited into their homes during the war.

Airmen, from whichever country they came, shared a collective sense of what looked best on the walls of their quarters.

Keep mum
she's not so dumb!
CARELESS TALK COSTS LIVES

Dances were a popular, and respectable way of meeting with the opposite sex, but for serving men it presented a number of perils too!

Cambridge was somewhat different. A few pubs crawled with Yanks, almost to the exclusion of the English. My crowd made a beeline for one of those, the Red Lion pub. There we would join a line, waiting our turn to order a 'Mild and Bitter'. A long 'queue' often stretched onto the sidewalk, and the bartender would be frantically doling out pints of warm sudsy beer. Impatiently, we would watch him fill the mugs with frothing, golden-brown brew and wait for the head to recede. In the process, he would take the head off with a wooden paddle, or the warm suds would spill over into the wooden trough below the spigot. The flat suds turned to beer in the trough and they were fair game to the bartender; periodically, he would take a pint mug and dip up the residue. To me, those were the 'dregs' to be rejected outright.

'Once our pints were in hand we would look for a chair and sit down; otherwise, we stood up, quaffed our pint of 'Mild and Bitter' and ogled the girls. On the whole, they were not the highest-class ladies. In spite of that, some of the men would pick them up to go dancing in the local dance hall or to fritter the evening away in the company of the opposite sex. I don't

BEWARE

HE WANTS TO KNOW YOUR UNIT'S NAME.
WHERE YOU'RE GOING. WHENCE YOU CAME.
EVEN ALONE OR IN A CROWD
NEVER MENTION THESE OUT LOUD.

By comparison......
A RATTLESNAKE IS HARMLESS

HE WARNS FIRST!

"LEAVE 'EM ALONE!"
DON'T BE A DOPE WITH A DOSE!

Pvt M. FRANKLYN

remember ever finding one that passed muster but sporting man that I was - I kept trying.

'The 'Six-by' back to the base left at 11:00pm so about 10:30 most passengers began to drift back to the parking lot where another display was to be seen, if there was sufficient light.'

Ernest E. 'Ernie' Russell,
adapted from *A Mississippi Fighter Pilot in WWII*

Socialising brought with it certain dangers!

COME BACK SOON

'Our crew and Granahans took the train over to Cambridge - about an hour's ride. One of the nicest towns I've seen in England. The Cambridge University and several other colleges are located there. It's a typical college town. The streets are crowded with students (most of them

These local girls appear to be more happy with their catch than do the Americans.

Love on a bar stool. 1940s wall art at Shipdham.

on bicycles) each with a book or two under his arm and a bright scarf around his neck. These scarves represent their individual schools and have the school colours. The graduating class also wears a black cloak. Saw a show and visited a few of the pubs. Didn't have time to visit Cambridge University. Hope to get back there soon.'

Diary entry, Andy J. Caroles, bombardier, 331st Bomb Squadron,
94th Bomb Group, Bury St. Edmunds

WHAT WAS THAT YOU SAID, MATE?

'I had gone to a party in Cambridge and had left late. I was scheduled to fly the next morning and didn't dare miss a combat mission. I got into a taxi and told the driver to take me to

The Red Cross set up hostels and clubs throughout the country, one of the best known being Rainbow Corner in Picadilly, London.

Honington. I went to sleep and when the driver woke me and said we had arrived I found we were in Huntingdon! He'd misheard my southern accent.'

Lieutenant Curtis Smart

FAVOURITE HAUNTS

'Free time for the troops was available once your plane was secured for the day. We had permanent passes to use when we were off. They just required you to sign out in the orderly room before leaving. A big 6 x 6 GI truck left the base at 6:00 pm for Cambridge and picked up between 11:00 and 12:00 pm for return to the base. Favorite GI haunts on base were The Sergeant Club, Duffy's Tavern, NAAFI-Red Cross Aero Club, Church Army and Betty and Bunty's Cafe. Just adjacent to the base were 'The Plough' and 'John Barleycorn' pubs in Duxford village, The 'Brewery' and the 'Waggon and Horses' pubs at Whittlesford Station and the 'Flower

The majority of Americans had to develop a taste for British beer, with its reputation for being weak and too warm.

Pot' in Little Abington. Towns farther afield were Hinxton, Sawston, Harston, Shelford, Thriplow Fowlmere, Great Chesterford, Foxton, Melbourne and Ickleton. Establishments the GIs were fond of in Cambridge proper included the Red Lion pub on Trumpington Road, Bull Hotel (Red Cross Club), Dorothy Cafe, American Bar, the Criterion and the Rex Ballroom. There we congregated with many of the bomber crews and hashed out the missions of the day, drank Mild & Bitter, threw darts and sang. The bars closed at 10:00 pm and after singing 'God Save the King', many of us queued up for fish and chips wrapped in newspapers at places that sold them. It was the best fish and chips I have ever eaten.'

James Tudor, crew chief, 78th Fighter Group at Duxford

PRETTY GIRLS

'Only once did I venture to another city besides Norwich and London. We spent a seventy-two-hour pass in Cambridge. I don't know what inspired us to go there. It was unlikely that we were thinking of our higher education there after the war was over Again, more sightseeing, visiting the university, some good eating and pretty girls.'

Major Frederick D. 'Dusty' Worthen

JUST MY CUP OF TEA

'Now at last, I told myself as I queued up at the counter, I shall get a decent cup of good English tea. My expectations rose even higher when I saw the woman behind the counter fill up the pot with hot water, so that the tea would be quite fresh.

It wasn't. It didn't even taste like tea. It was brownish in colour, with re-constituted milk and a minute portion of sugar in it, but it tasted as little like tea as army coffee tastes like coffee. At any rate, it was hot, which is all one could ask of tea or coffee in those days, and it served to wash down the rock cake and brace me for the crucial stage of my journey.

All this while, the Cambridge station was ringing with the voice of a female announcer, amplified over a loud speaker, who was calling the destinations of the trains in a voice of almost painful clarity and precision, dwelling with loving relish on each syllable. "The train-now standing-at number four-platform-is the four-seventeen train-for Ely-Lakenheath-Brandon-Thetford-and Norwich."

Suffolk Summer, John T. Appleby

ALMOST HEAVEN

'What can I say about Cambridge? How can I begin to speak of its beauty, to me the fairest on earth? First we went to King's college Chapel and heard Evensong. Where the boys' choir comes from I don't know, but it must be one of the very best in England. After the service was over we watched the choirboys in Eton collars and toppers, with umbrellas neatly furled, march out of the chapel, cross the Cam and disappear. 'Perhaps they live in trees, like the birds,' Bernard suggested. We had a long ramble through the colleges and then got a boat and spent a couple of hours on the river. I rowed upstream, while Bernard manned the tiller and we exchanged places coming downstream. It was one of those afternoons when one sees the English summer at its very best and I would willingly endure a fortnight of the worst of English climate has to offer, to be rewarded at the end of the day of such limpid perfection. The river was crowded with American soldiers who were snarling up traffic in a hopeless way, but the air was so full of good humour and high spirits that no one seemed to mind the immediate danger of capsizing.

Drifting lazily downstream we heard the bells of St. Mary's ringing the changes, while we saw the buildings at their most beautiful. It seems to me that I reached the very summit of human happiness during those sun-lit hours in the Cam.

We walked along the Backs beside the Cam with the warm spring sunshine lying like a haze over the river and the lawns and the mellow buildings. I walked through college after college, heedless of their names and in a trance of wonder at the beauty all about me. I am, I fear, given to strong prejudices. That afternoon I formed the conviction, strengthened by many subsequent visits, that if there is anything this side of heaven more beautiful than Cambridge as seen from the Backs on a sunny spring or summer day, I just don't want to see it. Cambridge will do for me.'

Suffolk Summer, John T. Appleby

Cambridge. Although taken a few years after the war's end, this photograph provides a reminder of how the city looked to the Americans.

War bride. Not surprisingly, many local girls opted for marriage and an eventual home in the USA.

'Before my train left in the afternoon, Iris and I walked around Cambridge. I thought about returning to that university some day, not because of Iris but because I knew that Cambridge was a great university. There was no renewal of romance with Iris and I had noted besides that she had some teeth that needed fillings.

Dancing with Iris, **Bob Shaver**

'Buzz and I were married in 1945 after he got back from England. We were both from the same small town, but hadn't dated until he came home from overseas. I'd written to several service men during the war and was familiar with V mail and sometimes mail had been censored and blacked out. So when Buzz showed me his diary he'd kept during months in England and I saw some of the things inked out I thought they were military secrets. For years I thought that until one day it dawned on me they weren't military secrets, but his secrets. After all those years to his dismay he couldn't remember what he'd blacked out... or so he said! In 1972 we made a trip to England; Buzz's and mine first since 1944. On a bus tour to Cambridge the tour guide told us we'd stop at 'Dorothy's Tea Room' for lunch. Buzz said that was where he used to hang out when he was on liberty. My response was, "You can tell your Mother you hung out in a tea room, but I'm not that gullible." Well, when we went up the stairs and I saw the bar and the ballroom in the back, I had to eat my words.'

Kay Fielding

MEMORIES ARE MADE OF THIS

MADINGLEY

'Doc was seeking a volunteer to accompany Pete's body to Cambridge. The day was beautiful and the long ride in ambulance was the first I had made through the English countryside. We drove a mile or two beyond Cambridge then turned off into a grove of trees alongside the road. Just beyond the grove was one of the neatest cemeteries (Madingley) I had ever seen. Under the trees were the chapel and other buildings, then sloping down to the northeast was the cemetery. Beyond the small stream in the valley bottom, the land rose again green and quiet.

The funeral was held two days later. The group provided us with a hard riding, cold six by six truck to travel to the cemetery. Besides the whole crew several of Pete's new friends from the other crews went. We left the base at 9 o'clock in the morning and travelled hours in bitter cold weather. We gathered a little way down the hill where each of us in his own way, then collectively, with the chaplain, prayed God to keep Pete near. There in the United States Cemetery, with the Stars and Stripes flying top cover, Peter Scott was buried. Pete's death robbed me of our invincibility and replaced it with guilt over his death and fear for the lives of the rest of the crew that I led into danger.'

1st Lieutenant Walter F. Hughes, 93rd Bomb Group

CRASH LANDING

'…Occasionally as medical officers, we had to travel with ambulance and driver to the Cemetery in Cambridge to carry our dead to their final resting place. On one such occasion as our ambulance travelled down one of those narrow English roads with high thick hedges on either side, the hedgerows suddenly erupted and a P47 hurdled across the road in front of us and came to rest on the other side the road. The ambulance driver stopped and I ran to the P-47, which was still intact and upright and climbed up on the wing. I was looking into the cockpit when the

Madingley Cemetery, Cambridgeshire. This is the only American Second World War burial ground in England. The 3800 white crosses and the Portland stone wall inscribed with 5000 names, pay tribute to the American servicemen and women serving in Britain who died in the war.

MARYLAND

One of the stained glass and engraved plaques at Madingley Cemetery commemorating those from the United States who fought and died.

pilot opened the canopy and looked at me. He apparently was unhurt for he spotted the caduceus on my blouse and said, "Doc, how in the hell did you get here in such a hurry?" He apparently had elected to make a belly landing after his fuel ran out.'

Frank J. 'Doc' Pickett MD, Medical Officer at 'Old Buck' from 19 April 1944

NEVER TO BE FORGOTTEN

'Seeing the B-17s forming up prior to a mission was a most spectacular sight to watch and hear. Planes from several airfields began the climb out and into formation before setting off. Even my

Boeing B17 Flying Fortresses lined up on an airfield indicate the sheer weight of armaments the Americans were able to bring into the war, particularly preceeding D-Day. Such spectacular sights would never be seen again.

headmaster allowed us to watch this event at 0900 hours when we should have been in school, commenting that this was 'something that you will never see again'. I lived about three miles from Grafton Underwood. When the wind was in a certain direction I could hear the B-17 engines being run up prior to a mission, then quiet for a short time. Then the engines revved again followed by the sound of brakes being applied, as they began to taxi to the runways. Engines roared about every thirty seconds as they took off.

My first recollections of the 8th Air Force was cycling a few miles to Deenthorpe airfield to watch the return of the 401st Bomb Group B-17s from their missions. Sometimes I noted the damaged planes as they came in to land. When two red flares were fired from an aircraft it signified that there were wounded aboard or perhaps something worse. Ambulances raced to the planes to attend to the injured as soon as they turned off the runway. Sadly, there were a few crashes near my home. Some were take off crashes and some mid-air collisions with many fatalities among the crews. I visited a few of these crashes and it was a very sad sight to see. I always thought that it was some mother's son who had died so far from their homes. In December 1944

US 8th Air Force insignia

B-17s over Europe, escorted by a P-51 Mustang fighter.

The old watch tower at Deenthorpe airfield. Demolished in the 1990s.

US trucks transported all the local school children (me included) to the base for a Christmas party. Bananas, ice cream, oranges and turkey were all on the menu. Quite a treat for us kids. We were each given a small toy made by the GIs to take home. Trucks then took us all safely home. How could I ever forget generous Yanks?

In later years I met two members of a B-17 crew that survived a crash on 5 December 1943. We became good friends and Ben Musser the radio operator invited us to visit his family in Tucson, Arizona. What memories I have, which included a visit to the Grand Canyon in 1989. Sadly he died in 2006.

In 1974 the 401st Bomb Group Association was formed and I became involved with them. Over the years I helped with their reunions in the UK. I held a private pilot's licence for many years and took several vets for a flight over their old airfields. Again a wonderful privilege for me to be entrusted to do this. What memories! I call them 'Nostalgic Flights' Now I help look after their memorial near their old base. I also lay a wreath every year at Madingley on behalf of the 401st Bomb Group. It is a great privilege for me and is always quite emotional.'

Paul Knight

A US Air Force Bomb Dump in East Anglia.

A B-24 is cut in half by rocket fire over Germany. Such was the grisly death met by so many American airmen who daily flew on combat missions in the skies over Europe.

ELY

'Ely and its cathedral dominate the level of the Fenland for many miles. The town is built on a rise and in former times was an island amid impenetrable marshes, through which the River Ouse was the only means of access. Indeed, so impenetrable were the fens that at the time of the Norman Conquest, Hereward the Wake and his company, together with the sturdy and independent Fen people, who refused to acknowledge the Norman invader, were able to hold out almost indefinitely against William's forces who got as far as Cambridge and then were baffled

Left: Ely Cathedral from the air.

Above: The Octagon of Ely Cathedral was built circa 1340 following the collapse of the original Norman tower. The eight massive wood pillars, 63 feet long with girths 2 feet 7 inches by 3 feet 4 inches, support 400 tons of glass and lead. A monk, Alan de Walsingham, was the architect for his incredible feat of engineering. The Memorial Window to RAF personnel in the cathedral replaced the 19th century glass in the western-most window of the North Aisle of the presbytery, which presented the story of St. John the Baptist.

by the trackless morass. The people of Ely were never overcome. In 1071, realising the futility of holding out against the entire country they came to terms with the King and acknowledged his sovereignty in return for his confirmation of all their ancient rights and privileges.

The great lantern of Ely Cathedral, supported by wondrous oak beams 65 feet long, can be seen from every part of the Isle of Ely, as that section of the Fenland is still called. Although the lantern is so called because it admits light to the interior of the cathedral, Mr. Jarman tells me that for many centuries it was a lantern in the true sense, with a light burning there at night to guide travellers across the Fens. Ely was the first English cathedral I had seen, and it seemed to me so beautiful that I could hardly believe it was real. There is a great deal of lovely Norman work in it, including the whole of the nave, and the chapel at the south-western corner, with the calm and severe serenity of its round arches, remains in my memory as the loveliest part of all. Norman strikes me as having achieved perfect balance and poise, effortless serenity and peace, while the later, pointed styles affect me as restless and constantly striving to achieve a balance they never quite attain.'

Suffolk Summer, John T. Appleby

PRESS BUTTON 'B'

'The telephone system is a constant bafflement. Not merely for the complexity of Button A and Button B but for the unpredictable results obtained from manipulating these gadgets and the familiarity with which he can converse with the unseen operator at the other end of the line. Accustomed at home to hear nothing from these impersonal, stylized voices that is not strictly business, he is amazed and often delighted to get advice, consolation, humour, back-chat and philosophy for his two pennies, even though he might fail to get though to his party. And strong rumour had it that in rare cases, if he knew the right words and the right sequence of questions, he might even get the age, colour of eyes and hair, approximate size, name and lastly a date with the smiling voice at the switchboard. This, definitely, was not the American way.'

First Impressions, Robert S. Arbib Jr.

HAIR OF THE DOG

'It was at 'The Dog' that we were officially welcomed to England... When we entered the little pub, it was almost empty. We found three or four small, plain rooms with wooden benches and bare wooden tables. Each room connected somehow with a central bar - either across a counter or through a tiny window. One of the rooms had a dartboard and another had an antique upright piano. We went into the room with the dartboard and ordered beer. "What kind of beer? "Asked the man behind the counter, a ruddy, pleasant man whose name was Mr. Watson.

"Oh just beer" we said. "Is this American money any good?" We conferred about the money and Mr. Watson finally decided to accept it after counsel with his wife, at the rate of four shillings to the dollar. He agreed to repay us later if the exchange proved to be higher, and he did. We tried the mild beer. It was weak, watery and warm. "Haven't you anything stronger?" we asked.

"They're all about the same now," he answered. "War-time quality, you know. Pretty weak." We tried the bitter. It was weak, sweet and warm. We tried the brown ale. We tried the stout. We tasted the Guinness. We ended by drinking the light ale, which was the only variety that seemed strong enough to put a foam on the glass. Later, we came to like or at least became accustomed to, the other types of English brew and would sit like the natives and talk over our pints of mild, or bitter, or 'aff and 'aff.

Someone must have seen us go into 'The Dog' for soon the villagers began to arrive. By ones and twos they came and sat themselves down in their accustomed seats. The front room with the dartboard filled with the younger men - the farm workers in their rough clothes, talking their musical dialect that puzzled us. In Norfolk they call it "Norfolk canary." But in Suffolk it is a twittering close-lipped sing song too.

This Saturday evening there was excitement and a high tempo in every room in 'The Dog'. The Yanks have arrived! There are seven of them in 'The Dog' right now! People came in from all the farms and cottages and they filled the old public house with a carnival spirit. By eight o'clock there was standing room only and by 9 o'clock even the dark narrow hall between the rooms was full and you could hardly turn around. The smoke was thick and the conversation excited.

The Yanks have arrived! The work on our aerodrome is about to begin at last! It has begun already! Right here, in changeless old Grunsbra we are going to have a great new bomber aerodrome and thousands of American soldiers and airmen! And bombers flying right over Berlin to pay those Jerries back! Surely the tide of war is turning today!

And so they flocked in. They questioned us and answered our questions and we listened to stories about the Blitz and heard about Dunkirk from men who had been there and we sat in the little back room with the piano and bought a round of drinks for everyone who joined the group.

First there were seven of us and then ten and then twenty-one drinks to the round and then twenty-eight. The last round we bought from the harassed Mr. Watson was for forty-seven drinks. There had never been anything like it before in the long history of' 'The Dog'. Everyone was shouting, everyone was singing and milling about, holding hands full of glasses over their heads as they pushed though the crowd. The word "Yanks" was on everyone's lips and if you turned away from someone it was to answer someone else shouting in the other ear.

Just about that time Mr. Watson raised his closing-time chant and a powerful call it was to cut though the din that rocked the rollicking old 'Dog ' that night. *"Time, please, Gentlemen!"* rang though the house like a brass gong and I suddenly realized with surprise what those lines in T. S. Eliot's "Waste Land "poem meant. *"Hurry up, please. It's Time!"* I heard that line a hundred times in dozens of public houses after that first night in 'The Dog' and I never quite got over the feeling that the publicans were quoting the poem and not the other way around.

That was our first welcome to England. We said goodnight to our new friends many times inside the pub and many times outside - and how we got home up the pitch-black country lanes to our tents in the Maze, I cannot quite recall.

We were the first of many American soldiers to spend a friendly evening with the light ale in the Grundisburgh 'Dog'. But 'none of the nights quite equalled the enthusiasm and abandon of that first visit of our gang. Mr. Watson told me that himself many months later.

That was Saturday night...that welcome at 'The Dog'. On Tuesday night 'The Dog' went dry - stone dry and Mr. Watson hung out a sad little sign on his door - "No Beer" - and closed his inn for the evening - the first time in 450 years of 'The Dog's' history.

The Yanks had come to England.'

Welcome At 'The Dog' from *Here We Are Together,*
The Notebook of an American Soldier in Britain, Robert S. Arbib Jr.

Favourite local inns around Debach airfield for 'pubbing' missions included the "White Hart" 'The Dog' at Grundisburgh, the 'Turk's Head' at Hasketon and the 'Greyhound' at Wickham Market. 'Odd these British pubs', wrote one chronicler in the 493rd Bomb Group. "They seemed to think that a pub wasn't worth walking into unless it was at least a century old, and nearly every Britisher would boast that his father, grandfather, and great grandfather had drank ale in the same pub, sitting in the same chair.'

Far right: While cigarettes and tobacco were rationed in Britain, the American Serviceman appeared to have an endless supply. Hence the remarks of a US airman: 'All the British smoke, from little brother and sister to grandpa and grandma, so that after an hour, many of the fellows claimed they needed a radar set to find their way through the fog to the bar. Practically all the ale was one kind or another of Tolly. A fellow didn't dare enter a pub without a good supply of cigarettes, because he would be hit up at least a dozen times an evening by "Gotta American cigarette chum?" Any time one was offered, it was always accepted.'

BAD COMPANY

'Johnny Ludwig was grinning at a tall, cross-eyed girl sitting across the room, who smiled back at him. But the old lady sitting almost in Johnny's lap warned him. "Stay away from that hussy," she confided. "She's got a bad name and a bad reputation. Went bad almost the day her husband went away to the Middle East. I know, I'm her mother-in-law."'

Robert S. Arbib Jr.

RACKHEATH

'The Air Ministry left on the base a crew of civilians headed by the Clerk of The Works. He was responsible for furnishing us with utilities. The electricity was direct current and presented all sorts of problems in converting for use with our American-made alternating current equipment. At the base dispensary much of the AC medical equipment did not function properly, even

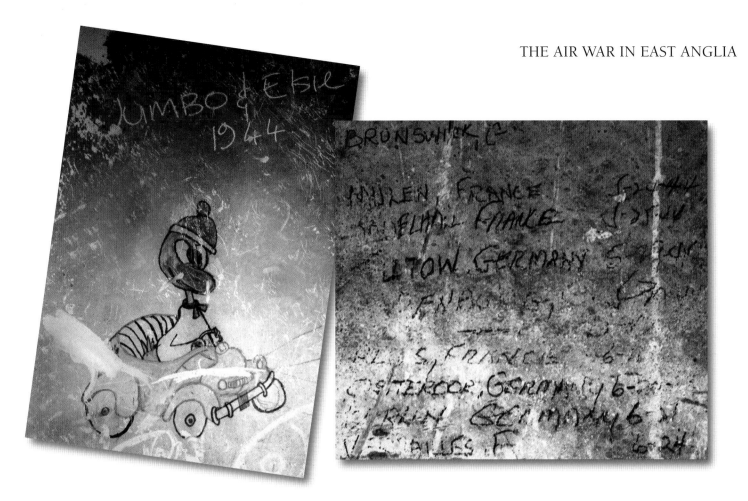

Graffiti and a list of missions flown over Europe found at Rackheath airfield.

when converted to DC. A memorable case in point was the dentist's drill. I first became painfully aware of it when I had to have some dental work done; they had gone back to the old fashioned man-powered field drill with its treadle arrangement lime grandma's Singer; one of the medics pumped away while the dentist drilled.

The Clerk of The Works also furnished our ration of coal and since that corner of England is cool and damp for a large part of the year, heating was a problem. The only source of heat in all our buildings was inefficient coal-fired space heaters. In the living quarters it was usually put to use in the early evening and was burned out before midnight. This meant that long under-wear went on before the end of October and didn't come off until after the first of May. It was usually worn for sleeping as well as waking hours and because of uncertain laundry service, inadequate bathing facilities and a pitifully short supply of hot water (also coal fired) they were not changed or laundered as frequently as we would have liked.'

Colonel James J. Mahoney, 467th Bomb Group at Rackheath 1944-45.

Newmarket racecourse.

NEWMARKET

'My first and only furlough in England began on an appropriate occasion, "Derby Day" and as an old improver of the breed with diplomas from Belmont Park, Jamaica and Aqueduct race-tracks on Long Island, I was determined to add a war-time Derby to my sporting experiences.

I caught the bus from Wattisham to Ipswich, the train from Ipswich to Newmarket and walked the remaining three miles to the site of the debacle. It was a warm June day and the sun shone and I was in one of those expectant moods - the somewhat elated, "*anything-might-happen*" mood that accompanies one to race-courses and then silently steals away immediately after the last race. In spite of travel difficulties there was a crowd of about nine thousand at Newmarket that day, all obviously in the same mood. They had come by train from London to Cambridge and Newmarket; some had hitch-hiked, others had walked and some had come on bicycles, of which there were hundreds stacked in fields beside the grandstand. …I rode back

Lincoln Cathedral.

to Cambridge that evening on the most crowded train I had ever seen. I rode standing up on the seat of the toilet in the lavatory. I couldn't even assume the dignity of a sitting position, for there was no room for my legs. We closed the door to make extra room for an additional passenger and that is how five racing enthusiasts journeyed from Newmarket to Cambridge. There were many, I think, less fortunate.'

The Sporting Life (Derby Day 1943) Robert S. Arbib Jr.

LINCOLN

'On Monday the 4th June I took the train to Lincoln and arrived there around noon. The Cathedral sits on top of a steep hill, and the great central tower is a landmark for many miles around. I toiled up the steep and narrow streets, too steep and narrow for any save foot traffic, and sat for a long time admiring the mighty west front, where one can see the first stirrings of the infant Gothic style. My first feeling, when I entered the interior, was one of intense disappointment. The stone is of such a harsh yellow, combined with the black Purbeck marble, that it offends an eye accustomed to the clear, mellow softness of the stone used at Ely and Norwich. My pet abomination, a huge organ at the crossing, blocked a comprehensive view of the whole and spoils the symmetry of the interior. However, in studying the Angel Choir and the interior of the great tower, my good humour returned.'

Suffolk Summer, **John T. Appleby**

Magnificent stained glass windows in Lincoln Cathedral.

Actor James Stewart also had a distinguished military career, flying many combat missions over Europe. In 1944, he became Chief of Staff of the 2nd Combat Bombardment Wing of the Eighth Air Force.

A FOGGY DAY IN LINCOLN

'I visited Lincoln on a foggy, rainy day and the cathedral, said to be one of the most perfect in England, was cold, damp and dark. Perfect it was, of a uniformity of design rarely found but of a style and a stone more ornate and less airy than the earlier Norman that I prefer, or the later, lacier Gothic that I like best of all. Of the other great cathedral cities of England, I visited Peterborough, Ely, Gloucester, Salisbury and Norwich and found in each beauty and inspiration. I saw the gaunt skeleton of the wrecked Coventry cathedral but I missed Winchester, Wells, York Minster and other famous ones. My favourite English church and perhaps one of the most spectacular sights in England, is Durham… travel difficulties and lack of time prevented me from visiting the south and west of England. But then, this never was intended to be a tourist guide!'

Tourist Days, Robert S. Arbib Jr.

CIDER AND CELEBRITY

'The limited supply of spirits allowed issuance per night of only two or three bottles of whiskey, two or three of wine and a keg of beer, plus soft drinks. The availability in the bar of Gaymer's Cider, made in nearby Attleborough, was akin to champagne and when mixed with beer was called "arf and arf" by its users. It made the beer much more potent. A radio and record player were wired to speakers in the three wings of the club and offered background music and news to those the reading room and the barroom. Rations were set aside for several weeks before the dance date. A list of the "good family girls" was wheedled out of the Red Cross in Norwich and formal invitations were mailed to them.

The event was epochal. The dinner participants were also touching in their open-eyed amazement at the prodigious piles of food served up in typical GI portions. None had seen so much food at one time during the many years of rationing. Some were seen to surreptitiously place the 1lb blocks of butter into their purses. No one could blame them. Hopefully, our generosity was not construed as another example of American braggadocio.

The presence of then Major James 'Jimmy' Stewart about this time on the roster, attracted a general and some of our "little friend" fighter jocks from the Groups that gave second Air Division their most welcomed attention - combat flight coverage. This dance ended at a reasonable hour, but the celebration continued less the female attendees, until the wee hours of the night…'

Old Buckenham dinner dance at the 'club' on base. Michael D. Benarcik

NORWICH AT WAR

THE TEN BLOCK RULE

'Riding my Raleigh bike on the way to lunch at Horsham St Faith mess I saw a very attractive blonde girl in civilian clothes come out of the Red Cross office. Having taken note, when I got to the mess I found one of the American Red Cross girls to ask who this attractive blonde I had seen might be. When told she was Joyce, an English girl working for the Field Director, I said that I'm in love already. She asked what I meant and I told her that I came from New York and when young, as my family didn't own a car, I only dated girls who lived no more than ten blocks away from my home. But for this one I'd make an exception. She laughed and said she didn't know if she could get me a date but would try. So she told Joyce about this love-smitten fellow, who laughed and said that she couldn't be bothered. Cupid's lot is not easily cast off so I suggested to the Red Cross girl, Jean Marshall, that if she brought a date I could invite Joyce to make up a foursome for dinner. She agreed and I phoned Joyce at her office and she accepted my invitation. Jean Marshall's date happened to be a young Captain who within a year became one of the top fighter aces in England. Joyce and I dated regularly after that and married 17 months later. I'm glad I made an exception to the ten block rule; the smartest move I made in my whole life.'

Jordan Utal, an officer with 2nd Air Division Headquarters near Norwich

NORWICH CATHEDRAL

'The Bishop's Palace had been converted into an American Red Cross Club and I had lunch there before going to see the Cathedral. Norwich Cathedral strikes me as not quite so lovely as Ely by which suppose I mean that there is less Norman there. Here I encountered for the first time the curious English habit of blocking the crossing of transepts and nave with a vast organ, which spoil the view into the apse and completely destroys the proportions of the whole build-

A lane leading towards Cathedral Close, Norwich c.1940.

The spire of Norwich Cathedral - the second tallest in England.

ing. This is all the more absurd and regrettable at Norwich, in that the organ has been destroyed by fire and it is only a painted counterfeit of building board, which spoils the symmetry of the interior. Even so, needless to say, there is much to admire there, particularly in the lofty apse with its first course of superb arches, and in the tracery of the arches in the cloister.

I spent most of the afternoon there and then went to the Church of St. Peter Mancroft to make a rubbing. At the door I was met by a woman who asked, "Bride or groom?"

Considerably startled, I replied, "Neither. I don't want to get married at all." Then I came to, as it were, and realised that a wedding was going to take place soon, and the woman wanted to know on which side of the church to seat me. I apologized for my absence of mind.

"The groom's an American soldier, too," the woman told me, "so we'll put you on his side. We'll certainly miss you chaps when you're gone," she confided as she showed me to pew. "Norwich won't seem the same without the streets full of American soldiers."

I sat through the wedding of an American sergeant to an English girl much prettier than he deserved, I thought, and then, having got the permission of the Rector and the Verger, I made a rubbing of the brass in the sanctuary.'

Suffolk Summer, John T. Appleby

FISH AND CHIPS

'Two days after our first mission we made the first of many trips into Norwich (pronounced Nor'ich) a city of probably 100,000 people. As one who always had a keen interest in history I found the city with its narrow, winding streets (some with centuries-old cobblestones) 900-year old Norman cathedral with the second tallest spire in England, eleventh century Norman castle and large open-air market to be a fascinating place. Even though it was winter, I was surprised to see fresh meat hanging out in the open in the market place. The supply of warm English beer was rationed daily and did not last long after the pubs opened their doors each evening. I bought my first fish and chips wrapped in newspaper from a street vendor and was surprised to find that the chips were not like our potato chips but rather were French fries.'

Staff Sergeant Dale R. VanBlair

UNDER THE BOMBS

'When war was declared in 1939 I was 15 years old and lived in a terraced house, 31 Belvoir Street, Norwich. My aunt was responsible for my upbringing after I'd lost my mother when I was 4 years old. One minute I was a schoolgirl, the next a wage earner! At that time, both my elder sister and younger brother worked in a shoe factory in Norwich. I had worked at the railway station for about a year when the city was bombed very heavily by the Germans in a series of quite devastating raids. Being near the East Coast we witnessed many low-level attacks by German fighters and bombers. When we could no longer hear the bombers overhead we

Mile Cross Bridge today.

ventured out into the street. Shocked, shaken and in tears, we saw an unbelievable scene of destruction. Most of the houses in Belvoir Street were damaged. A few had been reduced to scattered piles of fiercely burning matchwood and rubble. Many people had been killed, even more injured, some seriously. Other areas of the city had been hit much harder. By some miracle Number 31 appeared to have been one of the least damaged houses in the street, but it would be some time before we got our windows replaced and all the repairs completed. Many people were so apprehensive that they left the city during the nights, sleeping in any kind of shelter available in the surrounding countryside and returned to their homes the following morning. During the next seven or eight days after those two air raids, our family would leave our home after tea, walk out of the city, carrying blankets, pillows, sandwiches, hot tea in flasks and our torches to the Mile Cross Bridge and sleep under the bridge each night. We were up early the following morning, walked home and then went to our various places of work.

Nora Norgate's friend Ivy Seabourne, who was also brought up in Belvoir Street, loaned her wedding dress to Nora. Ivy, seen here in the dress at her own wedding, married Charles Holston, a cook in the 44th Bomb Group on 20 May 1944.

We'd become used to seeing strange-looking service men in Norwich from the early days of the war. When the 'Yanks' first appeared in the city in 1942 they were also very noticeable in their different style uniforms, and different language, which was English and yet it wasn't! For example, we'd never heard of a drawing-pin described as a 'thumb-tack." a torch as a "flash-light." nor petrol as 'gasoline.' Completely foreign!

I first met my husband-to-be Sergeant Herman Canfield in May 1944 at a friend's home near Wendling. He was a clerk in the Group Operations office. We got engaged in August 1944 and we were married at St. Phillip's Church in Heigham Road on 2 December 1944.'

Nora Norgate.

WARTIME NORWICH IN PICTURES

The photographs on the following pages are a reminder of how the city looked shortly before, during and after the war. They come from a variety of sources, including the photographs and drawings by Philippa Miller, daughter of a Norfolk boatbuilding family, who trained in dealing with incendiary bombs while also working as a part time ambulance driver in Norwich. A number of these illustrations appeared in her book *Norfolk Broads - The Golden Years* (Halsgrove 2008).

Above: *Norwich cattle market, with the castle behind.*

Right: *Norwich market on a busy day, pre-war.*

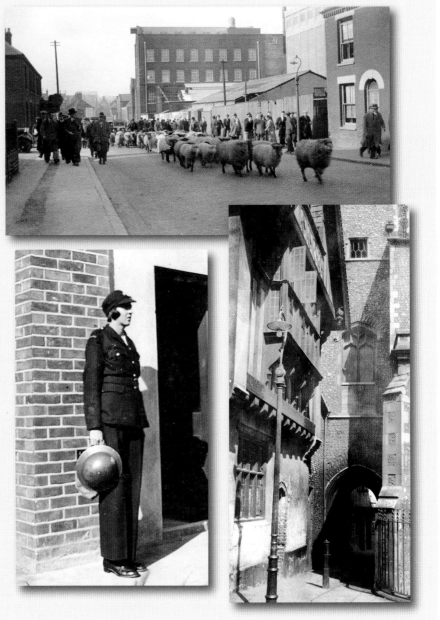

Above: *Pre-war Elm Hill, Norwich. Hitler deliberately targeted the most historic cities for bombing in reprisal for RAF raids on Germany. These became known as Baedecker Raids.*

Above right: *A flock of sheep being led along King Street, late 1930s.*

Right: *Philippa Miller in her ARP uniform.*

Far right: *The church of St John Maddermarket.*

PRACTISE PUTTING ON YOUR RESPIRATOR

1. Hold your breath. (To inhale gas may be fatal.) 2. Hold mask in front of face, thumbs inside straps. 3. Thrust chin well forward into mask. Pull straps as far over head as they will go. 4. Run finger round face-piece taking care head-straps are not twisted.

MAKE SURE IT FITS

See that the rubber fits snugly at sides of jaw and under chin. The head-straps should be adjusted so that they hold the mask firmly on the face. To test for fit, hold a piece of soft, flat rubber or of soft tissue paper to end of mask and breathe in. The rubber or paper should stick.

YOUR RESPIRATOR

COMPLETELY PROTECTS YOUR EYES, NOSE, THROAT AND LUNGS AGAINST ALL WAR GASES

ALWAYS KEEP YOUR RESPIRATOR SAFE, CLEAN AND EFFICIENT

IF YOU SUSPECT GAS, AT ONCE PUT ON YOUR RESPIRATOR AND GET UNDER COVER

Above left: Civil Defence ambulance crew at the Surrey Street depot in Norwich c.1941.

Above: Everyone was issued with a gas mask with orders to carry them everywhere, but not many liked to wear them.

Left: An interesting if motley crew of drivers and support staff at the Surrey Street ambulance depot, Norwich.

89

Left: *Philippa Miller painted this sketch of mothers picking up their vegetable rations at a makeshift grocery shop in wartime Norwich.*

Right: *One of a series of unique watercolour paintings by Philippa Miller portraying bomb damage in Norwich following the bombing raids of April 1942.*

Left: *The ruins of Curls Store and St Stephens Church, Norwich.*

Right: *A bath tub hangs from the shattered remains of a house in Oxford Street, Norwich*

Left: *Cayley's chocolate factory ablaze following a bombing raid on Norwich.*

Right: *A photograph of a wrecked classroom at Blyth Girls' School in April 1942.*

AT THE SIGN OF THE BELL

'First Lieutenant Max Sokarl invited Irving Goldman and me to meet him at the Bell Hotel in downtown Norwich one evening, saying that we were to meet some noted English philosophers. Like idiots, we went. I had never been in a Norwich hotel before and after seeing inside this one I was happy that I had no need to stay there. Not that it was an unpleasant place but one would surely not confuse it with the Hilton, nor even with the London Regent Palace…The Bell Hotel of Norwich was, according to Sokarl, the obvious spot to arrange a tryst, but it also required funding to schedule a room and it required the application of some sneaky tactics to thwart the nosy interference of the proprietors, who were self-appointed guardians of British Victorian morals. So Sokarl, taking advantage of the long, high-latitude, warm evenings of double British summer-time, would arrange to buy one portion of fish and chips to share with his paramour of the moment, then attempt to bed her down in a convenient countryside haystack. He had, so he claimed, found a particularly eager local nymphomaniac who took to haystacking like a duck to water. In fact, she often could not bother to wait for the fish and chips but would run down the road to the nearest pile of hay in order to get with it faster and with considerable energy.'

Jackson Granholm

The Bell Hotel, Norwich.

SAMPSON AND HERCULES

'Norwich, a city of 126,000 persons and the county seat of Norfolk, was the principal liberty city for much of the 8th Air Force. Personnel carriers left Hethel and dozens of other bases each evening after supper and discharged their cargo at Norwich, seven miles distant. They returned at 11 pm.

Tommy Volkman, a navigator from Streator, Illinois and I went to the Samson and Hercules, a dance hall that had been the city indoor swimming pool but was floored over for the duration so as to serve as a more interesting diversion for the American guests. By custom, the S&H had become the entertainment haven for officers; the enlisted men mostly habituated another dance hall. Tommy had already been there, and he would show me how to operate, he said. True to his word, he soon ushered me up to two girls and made wholly proper introductions to a blonde, Elaine Burt, and a brown head, Beryl Burt. We talked, and soon Tommy was off dancing with Elaine, probably without then knowing that she was a French-Canadian girl, married to Beryl's Royal Air Force brother, Joseph Burt. Left with Beryl, I soon got the idea that it would be quite proper for me to ask her to dance whether or not she wanted to.

Her face was not that of a Hedy Lamar and not even that of a Virginia Taylor. Rather, it had a distinct character. Years later, my father said her face was regal, like that of Queen Elizabeth.

I originally called Beryl "Bebe," as did her friends, the name being in reference to the initials standing for 'Beryl Burt." Bebe (Bee-bee) asked her mother if she could bring me to their home at 140 Earlham Road to meet her. For a time her mother said no. She didn't want any *bleedin'*

140 Earlham Road today.

The famous Sampson and Hercules pillars.

rich-love 'em-and-leave 'em Yanks in her house! In time however, Beryl defied her mother, Eva Nellie and brought me in unannounced. Her mother recovered nicely after being startled and it was not long before I gained her confidence. She liked me and I was different, she agreed, as Beryl had told her. "Being different" meant that I hadn't asked for the treatment that we Yanks often expressed, riding back to camp at night, a bit high in the personnel carriers, with these rollicking song words: Roll me over in the clover, roll me over, lie me down and do it again!"

Sometime in early 1945 it became evident to Eva that Beryl and I were very much in love, or should have been, considering the amount of time we spent together. One winter evening as the three of us sat watching a coal fire in the fireplace of their dining room, Eva said that she wanted to talk seriously with us; particularly me. It wasn't right, she said, for us to go on this way without Beryl or her knowing my Intentions. We probably ought to plan marriage - we had already discussed it - or stop seeing each other. Then, half-joking, she said, "I'm giving you a choice, you have to marry either Beryl or me."'

The Sweet and the Sour - Beryl and the War .
Bob Shaver and Beryl Burt married on 25 May 1945

LIFELONG FRIENDS

'At first English people seemed reserved and to avoid contact with us, but once the ice was broken they could not have been more friendly and helpful. Introductions were the problem. Mine came when we were putting on a show and wanted some civilian clothes for our girls and boys to wear on the stage. There was a canteen run by a women's voluntary organization at Blackfriars Hall, Norwich and I went down with the hope that someone could help me. The middle-aged lady I approached said she had a trunk at home full of old clothes and if there was something there we could use she'd be pleased to let us have it. So I got my driver to take us to her house Evelyn Thwaits became a good friend and thereafter I was often invited to her home. Our relationship lasted until she died.'

Hathy Veynar, one of the first WACs (Women's Army Corps) to reach the UK

Thousands of American women served in a variety of organisations in support of the fighting troops. Of these, many came to Britain and Europe as the war progressed. Over 150 000 women joined the WAC in the Second World War, the first women other than nurses to serve within the US Army ranks.

DOODLEBUGS AND DANCES

'I could usually only get to London once a month and there were attractions nearer to hand. When Jerry started launching buzz-bombs from out over the North Sea, the British moved in AA guns around our base, which was close to the coast. Several of these batteries were partly crewed by ATS girls. For we GIs it was like shooting fish in a barrel, there were so many of these girls at the social events. We also discovered the Palais de Dance at Lowestoft, a small port with a heavy Royal Navy presence. Fourteen of us went there to give a buddy who had volunteered for the infantry a good send-off. Whether it was the glasses of gin and orange or the GIs that attracted them I don't know, but we soon found we had a host of the navy girls, Wrens, round our table. However, my local attraction was an air force girl, a WAAF who was based at the radar directional station near Dunwich. She was single, a nice girl and good fun. Yes, I enjoyed my adventures in England.'

Art Swanson

WHAT A CHEEK!

'I started to go to dances when I was 16 years old and one Saturday night I went with some friends to the Oddfellows Hall at Weldon. The music was Glenn Miller, who was playing live over the radio. There were large windows in the hall with big sills on which we girls put our handbags. While I was dancing a group of Americans came in and sat on the chairs below the window where we girls had been sitting. When I went to get my handbag I said, "Excuse me, can I get my bag." And this Yank says, "I'll think about it." Cheeky so-and-so. Anyway, he asked me to dance to *In The Mood* and later he wanted to take me home. Now we girls had heard lots of things about these Yanks and were not sure what we might be getting ourselves into. So if you let one you weren't sure about take you home then the thing was to take him to the wrong house so he didn't know where you lived. My mother had no time for Americans but a few nights later she came in and said, "There's a Yank walking up and down the road outside with a torch and asking for you." As she was worried what the neighbours would think she told me to go out and ask him to come in. It was the same fellow and it was the start of our courtship.'

Stella Auger

SMUGGLING SPAM

'For a time I went with an English girl called Doris and she took me to her home. Her parents had me to meals and I could see this was putting a strain on their rations. Her father cut the roast in slices that were not much thicker than paper. So I used to try and take something from the base every time I visited. I'd smuggle out gallon cans of pineapple or spam in my knapsack. As you can guess, this made me popular. After a few weeks, when we were alone, Doris's father asked me what my intentions were towards his daughter. 'Honorable', I told him, but how could I tell him that you don't take a non-Catholic English bride home to a Polish mother.'

Stanley Sajdak

1953 ENGLAND REVISITED

Lieutenant Seward M. 'Mort' Meinstma, a Liberator pilot in the 785th Bomb Squadron, 466th Bomb Group at Attlebridge, Norfolk, flew 35 combat missions 25 August 1944 – 16 February 1945 piloting '*Slick Chick*' and '*The Flying Dutchman*'. He returned to England and to Norfolk in 1953 and took these wonderful colour transparencies of Norwich.

Left: R.T. Harvey's butcher's shop in Tombland

Right: Pedestrians and vehicles in The Walk

Left: *Tombland and the Maid's Head Hotel.*

Right: *Procession behind the Norwich Union coach past the Corn Exchange towards Prince of Wales Road.*

Left: *Purdy's Restaurant in Tombland, Norwich.*

Right: *Norwich Market.*

THE TIES THAT BIND

Right: *Memorial stained glass window at Grafton Underwood.*

JITTERBUG BALL

'I was dating someone from HQ who entrusted me to American serviceman Keith Vorhees for the dance at Metfield village hall. When I found Keith was a natural at the jitterbug things went from there.'

Edith, who married Keith Vorhees

MISSION BY BIKE

'Not many people can bless the day they broke a foot, but I can. Some horseplay during cadet pilot training resulted in this injury, putting me two months behind the rest of my class. Most went to Italy but I eventually ended up at Grafton Underwood. Shortly after my arrival I attended a dance and noticed a pretty girl on her own who appeared to be somewhat uncomfortable. After asking her to dance and getting acquainted, it turned out she had been stood up by another Grafton airman. I then started bicycle missions to Kettering nearly every evening. Couple of weeks later she found out that the man who dated her for the dance hadn't shown up because he broke his foot that afternoon and was in the base hospital. So one broken foot sent me to Grafton Underwood and another broken foot started a partnership that resulted in four children, seven grandchildren and on.'

Bill Barnett, 384th Bomb Group

RELIGIOUS DIVIDE

'I was one of the first men at Bassingbourn to have an English bride. I didn't drink and was having tea and sandwiches at some function in a church hall and got talking to a girl in British

Bassingbourn airfield today.

Army uniform, the ATS. When I asked for a date she backed off and said that I better write her a letter to ask! Never met such a shy girl. Well, eventually she accepted my proposal of marriage but the chaplain was told to try and talk me out of it. Don't think the US Army was too keen on its men marrying foreign girls at that time. To complicate matters I was Catholic and my future wife Protestant. In the end the chaplain was convinced I knew what I was doing and said go ahead. The chaplain on my wife's ATS base also had a long talk with her.'

Robert Cayer

PORTENT OF DEATH

'A pilot was having problems completing his missions. He was convinced that if he stayed with his Squadron he would be killed so he asked his squadron commander to move him to another Group. He was told that if he moved, others would wish to follow so he had to stay. He was sent to a rest home for a week and reported back to his squadron commander and notified him he still wished to move. His request was refused and told that he was detailed for a mission next day. His bunkmate was a staff officer who worked in the control tower. He called in to see him and told him that if he were killed he would come back to haunt the tower. Next day over the target the pilot was killed.

Wimpole Hall near Bassingbourn. In the Second World War this imposing mansion, now a National Trust property, dates back over 300 years. The house was used as a Rest and Recuperation Hospital by the 8th Air Force.

Many years after the war the chairman of a branch of the British Legion visited the tower, which was now a museum, to take photographs for his granddaughter, who was using the history of the airfield as part of her O level exams. He came out of the tower in a hurry looking rather pale and told staff that he had seen a figure dressed in World War II American flying clothes. He was also unable to operate his camera. Others claim to have seen this ghostly figure.

A gentleman from the North of England phoned to say he had an officer's hat given to his father who worked on the airfield during the war in return for some eggs. He was invited down and the hat was produced. The name in the hat was that of the officer who had requested a move from the group at the airfield.'

Anon

'GOING HOME'

'GOING to Boston! I was going to Boston! As the automobile sped across the level landscape on a road that was raised above the fields, now ploughed and waiting for winter, I tried to justify the excitement that filled me. For by now I was no newcomer to England…The first reason for that longing was the picture in my mind of the tower of St. Botolph's Church, known far and wide as the Boston Stump. For four years I had lived under the shadow of its replica in America, the lovely Harkness tower in New Haven. For four years I had admired that tower in sunlight through the tracery of spring-green leaves and in winter black against a sodden sky. I had known a pair of pale barn owls that had haunted that tower and I had listened to its carillon

102

each evening, ringing out the slow melody of the fine old spiritual that we know as " Goin' Home." So this was a pilgrimage in one way, a pilgrimage to the Boston Stump, under whose alter-shadow I had studied and dreamed of long ago.

…It was almost evening this November day. It had been a sunny day; only now were clouds growing in the sky, which still held a wan winter glow, when we first glimpsed the "Aould Stoomp." Caught in a last shaft of sunlight that could not reach the earth beneath, it shone across the fens like a white beacon lighting our way. So it must have looked to those other older pilgrims who, not coming to Boston but leaving it, had seen it shining across the fens thee hundred and more years ago.

We were going to Boston this day because the town had invited the American Army to celebrate the Thanksgiving holiday as their guests. A hundred soldiers were coming. They would attend a service in St. Botolph's Church, where the Archbishop of Canterbury would preach the sermon. They would dine at the Assembly Halls, Boston homes would be open to them and there would be a dance in their honour.

We came into Boston that evening in the darkening twilight and it had been market day. Just as I bad dreamed it the old houses stood about the square - and there was the statue to the local hero, the windmills by the canal, the carts and stalls now departed but a flock of sheep still stumbling though the Little Bargate. And dominating all the grand old Stump floating up against a now-lowering, racing sky.

The imposing tower of St. Botolph's church, Boston.

Inside the church November sunlight filtered through the windows and fell in gauzy gold on the garden of colour that filled the floor. Not a seat was vacant and behind the seated congregation the people of Boston were standing. Here were blocks of olive drab, of navy blue, or brown, air force blue, of tan and here and there a spot of white, or black. The choir lifted its sweet chant, the organ rolled, the words of the prayers and the sermons echoed bell-like through the church. Here, I thought, is the pure essence. Here is the return of John Winthrop and his company - the pardon, the blessing, the warm welcome. Here we were united again, working and fighting and now praying side by side - celebrating here in England an American holiday. And when by some quirk of fate the organ pealed the strains of "Goin' Home," I was back in Connecticut again; there was no Atlantic Ocean and for that moment no difference at all between old England and the new.'

Thanksgiving At Boston (1943), **Robert S. Arbib Jr.**

BLIND DATE

'During total blackouts it was commonplace for all entrances to have a curtain to prevent any light leaking out. We were told, "The tiniest of lights could be seen for miles from the sky." When the curtain of the pub was pulled back, I got the shock of my life and I wanted to kill my friend on the spot. My date was at least thirty years my senior and one of the ugliest women I had ever seen. The ugly witches I had seen in pictures and in the movies couldn't hold a candle to this woman. One look at my-used to be-friend, (who had the beautiful English girl I had seen in pictures) told me he wanted to crawl in a hole. And at that point I would have been more than willing to dig for him and cover him up after he crawled in.

Although the pub was crowded, it seemed to me every eye was on my blind date and me. One Englishman nudged me as we passed by and said, *"Blind date, eh Yank?"*

The walk back to the shuttle bus was spent with my ball-turret gunner making excuses and apologies to me, which I accepted. But I told him from then on I'd meet and pick out, my own dates. When we returned to base and everyone asked, *"How was your blind date?"*

We both lied and said, *"She was a beauty!"*

Lieutenant Dan Culler

WINDING TO WYMONDHAM

'I managed to draw a bicycle from the supply office. The base was so spread out it was difficult to get around without a jeep or a bike. The English summer was at its height, though it never really got warm enough according to my idea of summer. The air was fresh and cool, like a day of spring at home and the woods, which were scattered all over our airdrome were beautiful. Through the woods small lanes were cut leading to the various living sites. I found in those first days in England many of the acquaintances of my early years: there were rooks and jackdaws flying overhead and grouse, plover and pheasants in great numbers just off the runways.

The second afternoon I was in England, I rode my bike into the small village of Wymondham (pronounced Windum) near the field and was impressed by its picturesqueness. The lane leading into the village was narrow and winding, with hedgerows on either side and well-kept fields over the hedgerows. There were haystacks in the fields that were so perfectly formed they looked like loaves of gingerbread.

On the edge of the village was a little pond with ducks on it. Farther on the streets were narrow with brick buildings almost to the edge of the pavement. They seemed particularly incongruous when an occasional tremendous American Army truck lumbered through. At the far end of the town was a very old church that looked as if it might have been started as a Stonehenge in pagan times and continued having parts added down through successive ages of Christianity. The whole scene had a kind of beauty strange to me.'

Philip Ardery

Abandoned bikes on an American airbase.

LEFT HAND DRIVE

'I was heading for *The Dog* pub one evening. Hadn't met any traffic so, not thinking, was riding my bike on the right-hand side of the road as if I was back in the States. Suddenly a lorry comes round a corner, head-on towards me. I dodged out of the way by pedalling off the road, finishing up in a bramble bush.'

Ivan Brown, Halesworth

CITY LIGHTS

"Well first the bloody Jerry's got to find London in a blackout, then he has to find Neasden,
then he has to find number twelve Cheltham Court and then I'll probably be
down at the pub havin' me pint."

'I love the uproarious good humor of the Cockneys. These people are a breed apart - quite unlike any of the other English that I have met. Hitler's bombers could not break these people's spirit. They really thrive on adversity. One cannot help but wonder if there are people in Germany who have thrived on the nightly bombing from the RAF. Somehow I doubt that in German beer parlors there is a Cockney equivalent standing up singing while the bombs fall…but there in the pubs of London that is exactly what they do…'

Colonel Harold Richard Hennessey, letter home, August 1944

LONDON REVERIE

'At St. James's Palace a guard in battle dress emerged from his box, clattered, walloped and banged his rifle, flipped it here, flipped it there, stamped about and presented arms. I was the lone witness to the performance; he could have carried it out only in my honor. I was as embarrassed as if I had broken wind in Westminster Abbey. I saluted smilingly. Unsmiling, he reversed the process, unwinding himself rhythmically to his original position.

As clearly as I beheld that guard on solitary parade, I saw Charles I ride down Whitehall past the Admiralty building with its bare-branched forest of aerials to lay his head on a black-draped block. There were ducks and governesses and seedy men with stained mustaches sipping their morning tea in the park across the road from Charles's Scaffold.

A yellow August haze cloaks these recollections of London during the frantic twenty-four-hour passes, which we snatched between battles. From the Victoria Embankment near the

Along the Embankment, London.

monument to abolitionists with its playful gimcrackery I watched the shaggy tugs snorting like buffaloes. And I looked longingly at American tankers. On these vessels, available to airmen who could talk their way on board, were sumptuous steak topped with eggs, such as were found nowhere else in England or in any army mess except the rear-echelon top-Brass hostelries at Wing or SHAEF.'

Elmer Bendiner

PUTTING ON THE RITZ

Tea at The Ritz.

'Once a month we were given a two- or three-day pass to London. We did get to see Piccadilly and a bunch of other sights of London, although I must admit I wasn't in London looking for sightseeing. We would look for bars and good food and we would have tea at the Ritz where we could dance. It was just getting away - from the bombing and planes going down and from that kind of stuff. This was an interesting episode, because London was blacked out and was constantly being bombed. The Germans were sending over their buzz bombs, which had just enough fuel to go just so far and then would head down to the ground, which is why they were called "flying bombs." We were in a hotel one time and a wing of that hotel was hit by a flying bomb. It scared the hell out of us and in fact, after that, I decided I would rather go to Cambridge. Both because it was a university town and didn't involve a long train ride and, also, because I didn't see any sense in going to London and risking being bombed. We usually wound up at Dorothy's, a dance hall on the second floor of an old building in Cambridge.'

August Bolino, navigator, 388th Bomb Group, Knettishall.

COSMOPOLITAN LONDON

'LONDON during these months was one of the worst crowded cities of the world and one of the most fascinating. It was full of people during the week days and on weekday evenings. It was even more crowded on Saturdays and on Saturday evenings it was almost bedlam, especially in those parts of town where Americans on leave congregated. I always thought of London as the hub of the world in those days. Here was not only the throbbing heart of the British Empire but here too was the capital-in-exile of half a dozen other nations. Here the strategy and plans were being conceived, from here the vast armed forces were being marshalled and directed and on London were the eyes of the world. Battered and dirty, worn and scarred, it swarmed with scores of different uniforms and it spoke in a hundred different tongues. No matter where you were going in the United Kingdom, you had to go through London and no matter how long you stayed you never saw it all. London was the Babel, the Metropolis, the Mecca. London was It.

The centre of London on a Saturday night was Piccadilly Circus. Here was a microcosm of the whole - a combination of crossroads, entertainment centre, restaurant centre and meeting-place. Here was a bawdy, rowdy anthill that moved in thee dimensions and on four levels and in a dozen different spheres. You could not see it all at a glance - it was a shifting kaleidoscope

Life in central London carried on despite the blitz, but the real toll of the Blitz was the devastation of thousands of buildings, the effect only obvious once clearance had begun.

that only now and then came sharply into focus and then blurred again, leaving fleeting images on the mind. Piccadilly hail everything.

It had soldiers, sailors and airmen in uniform, looking for fun. Americans, British, French, Canadians, Norse, Poles, Belgians, Czechs, Dutch - you could run down a roster of Allied nations and find all their representatives here in a moment or two. The Americans surged in a never-ending tide around the Rainbow Corner - milling theft way in and out of that mammoth beehive, in search of friends, food, dancing, of an hour's sleep before a train left, or of a bed for the night.

From the Rainbow Corner the Americans flowed out and around the Circus. Some were in search of restaurants and theatres. Some were in search of bars and beer. Some were looking for girls.

The girls were there - everywhere. They walked along Shaftesbury Avenue and past the Rainbow Corner, pausing only when there was no policeman watching. Down at the Lyons' Corner House on Coventry Street they came up to soldiers waiting in doorways and whispered the age-old questions. At the Underground entrance they were thickest and as the evening grew dark they shone torches on their ankles as they walked and humped into the soldiers, murmuring, "Hello, Yank." "Hello, soldier." "Hello, dearie!" Sometimes they were drunk and then they would stand and shout at each other and sometimes come to blows. Around the darker estuaries of the Circus the more elegantly clad of them would stand quietly and wait - expensive and aloof. No privates or corporals for these haughty demoiselles. They had furs and silks to pay for.

Servicemen and women mix with civilians outside a cinema.

Down in the Circus, standing on the kerb, were the men who pretended to sell newspapers. *"Poybeeb! Poybeeb!"* they shouted, *"News... Standard...Star!"* But if you walked close to them you could hear them mumble about something else they were selling and if you asked them for a newspaper they turned and growled, *'G'wan beat it!'* There were other salesmen too. There was always a man who came up to you and offered to sell you a bottle of whisky for four pounds or more. There was the man who could take you to a "bottle-party" where you could drink and dance as late as you pleased. And there was the man who would buy your fountain pen.

The people surged everywhere. At the Newsreel Theatre they look at the framed pictures on the billboard for a moment and then went in to pass an hour. At the Brasserie across the Circus they looked askance at the burly doorman and ducked in for a quick meal. At the shop across the street there were huge sandwiches of meat pastes - or was it fish? At the "Swan and Edgar" corner two ATS 'polite' girls stood with red bands on their hats - prim, austere, guardians of the gentler sex in uniform. Bobbies, too moved among the crowds, their coalscuttle hats standing above the heads of the people. In pairs and in fours the white-helmeted American police patrolled the streets and the girls whispered at them CC Snowball!" There were frowsy women who lurched along in a private dream muttering to themselves, and beggars playing the violin for pennies at the theatre queues. There were people standing in the streets shouting at taxis that would not stop.

Picadilly Circus.

There were little bars and public houses down Denman Street and Dean Street where the prostitutes drank and got drunk and forgot their profession, to wander home alone to their little rooms in the alleys back of Tottenham Court Road. There were the shiny, brightly-lighted restaurants in the hotels where bands played and the atmosphere was sultry and the waiters were dressed in black and the bill was large. Up on the roofs of these buildings there were lonely men and women standing on fireguard waiting for the sirens and the bombs that might follow them.

Down below the ground, too, the activity is intense. On the first level of the Underground there are swarms of people moving in all directions, people waiting by the telephone booths and pondering the ticket-machines. This is where you kiss your girl good night and where the sailors burst into song and where the military police stop soldiers and ask to see their passes.

As you take the long escalator down to the second level there is always someone sitting on the moving steps and always a Canadian soldier who is lost. And then the third level where the wind blows dust in your face and more steps to run down and then the fourth level, hundreds of feet underground, where the trains run to Watford. Here is Pat in her grey smock, with her back to the tracks, hands in her pockets, running the show. "Stanmore Line! All stations to Stanmore! No, this is not the Watford train! Hurry up, please, there! Step lively now! Mind the *Doors!* Mind the doors, please, there! Stanmore train! Last train to Watford is 11.37. Hurry up, please!

Pat stands there by the hour, being shoved and pushed and yelled at and not too tired to have her little joke. "Austerity travelling there," she shouts. "Move right down in the cars, please!"

There's the tall, blonde girl in an evening wrap who suddenly breaks into an operatic aria down in that windy tunnel! Everyone stops to listen and when she finishes they all applaud- even the austere old British colonel! And when the Watford train comes at last, there's a fellow in the car playing a violin. Just playing it for music, not for money. And when he leaves at Baker Street, a sailor comes in and starts to sing. He dances up and down the aisle, favouring each passenger with a tune and a smile and soon everyone is singing together. "I'm Just a Little Sparrer," we all sing. And "Dear Luvverpool!" and "I Belong to Glasgow" and "Nellie Dean." We all sing, the moustached nun in spats with the silver-topped cane, the labourer with the smudged face and the burlap bag on the floor between his legs, the four sailors and the French soldier who doesn't know the words, the sentimental middle-aged lady and the little fellow with the big pipe. They all sing, all but the lovers in the middle seat. They just sit and hold each other tightly, the girl looking up at him dreamily, lost in clouds. They hear nothing, they are far away; - this RAF pilot and his girl.

As the bars and public houses close there is a brief flood of people again. This is the second of three tides. The first came when the theatres emptied their crowds at half-past nine. The "Closing Time" crowds are the second. And the third will come an hour later with the rush for the last train home. After the last trains leave, there are still a few girls walking the streets, still a few maudlin groups of soldiers - like-as-not lost, like-as-not unconcerned about it -progressing with determination toward some uncertain goal. In the dark shadows of Air Street a soldier leans against a doorway and goes to sleep. Down in Great Windmill Street a late lingering girl, quite drunk, tries to convince a timid airman to come home with her - for seven quid.

Now and then the pale blue glow of lights moves though the streets and disappears to a chorus of "TAXI!" from all sides. Piccadilly Circus is almost though for the night now. There are a few night clubs open, if you have the money and know where they are. But they are hot, noisy, cheap - their music is bad and the liquor that you must buy by the bottle tastes like the bottom of a tanning vat.

The Circus is almost quiet now. In the distance a pale grey 'S' hangs from the doorway of a shelter and the tiny lights on the avenue click from red to green but the rest is darkness. The wind blows scraps of paper and refuse across the pavement and in the distance you can hear the piping note of a policeman's whistle. On the corner of Shaftesbury Avenue are two sailors and two girls singing. One of them has an oil lantern in his hand. He walks out into the precise middle of the street, swinging his lantern from side to side and he urinates.

This is London at war, this is England-or a small part of it - with its hair down. Piccadilly - dirty, maudlin, tumultuous - fascinating, obscene.

Good night, Piccadilly - time to call it a day.'

London After Dark, **Robert S. Arbib Jr.**

Big Ben and the Palace of Westminster.

MISTAKEN IDENTITY

'One time, in London by myself looking for a good place to eat, I went into one of the major hotels. As I went by the doors there were a couple of our MPs walking up and down the street. I sat down and was about to order when a waiter comes over and says, "*There's an MP who would like you to join him.*" Well the first thing I thought of was the two MPs I'd seen out there, so I said I don't want anything to do with MPs and if they want they can come and talk to me. The waiter went away and didn't approach me again. I had my meal and left. I got to wondering why an MP should want me. It was only later that someone suggested that the MP was a British Member of Parliament. I've often wondered what I missed and that I might have left a bad impression of GIs' courtesy if it was a British politician.'

Wilbur Richardson

The London Underground became a nightly dormitory for hundred of families escaping the bombing. Shown here is Elephant & Castle tube station.

SLEEPING QUARTERS

'Altogether, most of our crew went on pass to London about four times. We usually stayed at the Regent Palace Hotel overlooking Piccadilly Circus in the heart of London. All the windows had been blown out of one side of the building and were replaced by wooden shutters. Another vivid memory of London consisted of the evenings we took the tube (or underground subway), to the enormous dance hall known as Covent Garden, an opera house dating back to 1732. There, on the concrete subway floors in full view of passersby, whole families spread out their blankets in preparation for a night's sleep. These were the bombed out poor of London and they had been living like this in the subway for several years since the London Blitz.'

The Year I Can't Forget, James E. O'Connor

LANGUAGE DIFFICULTIES

'We arrived at Liverpool Street Station without mishap and decided to take the tube downtown. This was a mistake, as none of us had learned to speak the language and it was practically impossible to communicate with the natives. We lost Junior on the tube and didn't see him 'till we returned to the base.'

Bill Carleton, 351st Bomb Squadron Engineering Officer, 100th Bomb Group

FRESH FRUIT

'The 'tube' was the most memorable and wonderful technology for people that I encountered in my entire stay in England. The trains and stations were amazingly clean, given the circumstances…the ends of some subway lines came to the surface in residential areas and I enjoyed seeing the suburban homes with their small gardens. On one trip I rode up the escalator behind a mother and four or five year old daughter. I gave the little girl an orange I brought from the base. She curtsied and said, "Ta", turned to her mother and asked, "What is this mama?" The mother said with tears in her eyes, "She's never seen an orange before".'

1st Lieutenant Walter F. Hughes

OUTNUMBERED!

'…A city of pomp and splendour, a panorama of history, theaters, restaurants, some of the best pubs in England…and plenty of girls. You could go to a dance in Covent Garden and find a ten to one ratio of women to men and fifteen to one of women to Yanks…For the less adventurous, there was the Red Cross Rainbow Corner Club. The neighborhood had a questionable reputation, being in Piccadilly Circus and frequented by ladies of the night dubbed 'Commando's'. The club was a big help to the GI. Fred Astaire's sister, Lady Cavendish, who was a regular volunteer…writing to servicemen's families and a host of other activities. She even got a bottle of scotch for us…well it was for Jack Lang; she didn't trust the rest of us to deliver it.'

December, W. J. 'Red' Komarek

Poor diet led to the danger of illness and infection. The Ministry of Health coined this famous phrase used on this poster.

BOMB DAMAGE

'Before noon I had completed a whirlwind tour of the main items of interest, namely, the Houses of Parliament, Westminster Abbey and Buckingham Palace. Alongside Parliament I gazed at Big Ben, but didn't hear it chime. A guide led me through the Abbey, showed all the graves of famous scientists, poets, statesmen and kings I'd read about from the first history class on. I walked alone through St. James Park, along a pond filled with paddling ducks and herons, to Buckingham Palace…Then to Grosvenor House officer's mess and on my way to the Tower of London, where a tour had been arranged for soldiers. I stopped off on the way to listen to a band concert on the steps of St. Paul's Cathedral and then went inside for a quick look before going

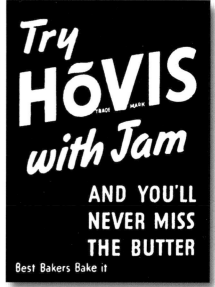

Try
HŌVIS
TRADE MARK
with Jam
AND YOU'LL
NEVER MISS
THE BUTTER
Best Bakers Bake it

Most American servicemen were genuinely shocked by the living conditions endured by ordinary Londoners. Bombed out of their homes, eking out meagre rations, life in England was poor compared to the conditions many had enjoyed back at home. The Ministry of Food waged a constant battle against waste, providing information on how best to make the most of each meal.

Londoners on their way to work through Blitzed streets. The damage remained long after the war had ended.

to the tower. Saw where a 500 pounder had landed inside the Cathedral during the blitz. Quite a bit of damage.

Along Cannon Street, leading to the tower, I had the opportunity to see what great damage the blitz had done at its worst. An area, blocks wide and long, had been completely devastated, not even a chimney left standing. The Jerries must have laid their heavies there. Grass grew in what had once been warehouse cellars…All the while I saw these never-to-be-forgotten places, I wished with all my heart that someday I might again see them all again with Mary. There's nothing like appreciating both the sights and the light in her eyes at the same time - that's appreciation. Alone, I could see but do not share, nor appreciate.'

Claude V. Meconis

BUZZ BOMB

'Thousands of Londoners spent their nights in the 'tube" or "underground," as they referred to their subway system. They brought blankets and slept on either cots with wire springs or the walkways. When Pete and I took the tube back to the hotel late each evening, we found

'Hey Paw. Tell me again how you and the boys were sweatin' it out in the ETO.' This mural, found at Shipham airbase, is gently self-mocking of the American airmen, suggesting they spent their days enjoying wine, women and song.

hundreds of people sleeping there. I developed a great deal of admiration for these people who could spend their nights under such conditions and then put in a full day's work. Although the blitz was long since over, German bombers still put in an occasional nuisance appearance over London and other cities. When I saw the evidence of the damage done during the blitz, I could only marvel that the Londoners' morale did not break. The whole area around St. Paul's Cathedral, for example, was practically leveled, as were many other areas. On a later trip to London, I found that the top floor or two of our hotel had been destroyed by a buzz bomb.'

Staff Sergeant Dale R. VanBlair

AT THE FLICKS

'Big Ben, Houses of Parliament, Westminster Abbey, Buckingham Palace, Tower of London and St. Paul's Cathedral were the sights to see. It was dinnertime when I finished and I took in a movie afterwards. It was *A Guy Named Joe* with Spencer Tracy, Irene Dunne and Van Johnson, a good "flick" that I'd already seen three times before.'

London Town, Lieutenant Truman J. 'Smitty' Smith, co-pilot, 385th Bomb Group, Great Ashfield, Suffolk, May 1944

'

TOWARDS THE END

A SORRY PLACE

'Approximately 12 miles from the coast and close to the River Stour. The inter war farming depression had not been kind to the area and the way of life and bygone age was still very much in evidence. When we arrived the Raydon station was a 'sorry place' if the expression may be used. The base was built by American Engineers who follow the British plan of a station and simply do the construction work. The workmanship is not up to our standards and certainly not up to British standards in any way… The surrounding countryside is beautiful with its sloping hills yet poorly constructed Nissen huts marred its beauty. The masonry is particularly bad. One can easily see through the cracks between the bricks and feel the cold breezes blow through the cracks around the window sills. It is not uncommon to have a leaky roof. …Many have jokingly called the Group the 353rd Engineering Co. However, when we saw the mess we were moving into, everyone said, 'changes will be made when the 353rd moves in.'
  Captain Ernest MacGregor, 353rd Fighter Group, 13 April 1944

FUN ON THE BROADS

'Before Christmas, the Watkins crew flew one practice mission to test some new equipment or procedure. It was a beautifully bright fall day in East Anglia. At the close of the mission, we were over the Norfolk Broads, an expanse of lowlands that only recently, in a geological sense, emerged from the North Sea. It was in fact a resort and pleasure area dotted with windmills, lakes and a network of interconnecting canals. On this particular day it was also dotted with pleasure yachts. Tom thought it would be great fun to buzz the broads and perhaps rock a few yachts from our following draft. Of course, it would also be fun to skim the lake or canal, pretending to be a hydrofoil, head straight for a yacht and pull up at the last moment. We might even see the 'Gaw Blimey' occupants hit the water.'

Bob Shaver

'Today has been beautiful out, Vonny, just like summer almost…We've been figuring on whether or not to get a yacht for the summer, and this afternoon, Nat and Frank went down to the Broads to see about a boat. There's about 200 miles of river around here to sail on, and it's not far from here so that most any evening we could go up by bike. On a two-day pass we figure we could have a swell time with a 16 or 20-foot sailboat. After talking it over, the five of us have about decided to invest in a 3-bed, 24-foot yacht. It's going to cost us each about two pounds a week, but we figure it will be worth it just for the fun and relaxation.'

MESSING ABOUT IN BOATS

'A popular British pastime in Norfolk was to go sailing in small sailboats along the canals and small streams. This pastime prompted us to develop another sport of trying to blow over or capsize these boats while on training flights. On one occasion we made a couple of passes but couldn't capsize one, so we made another pass very low and directly at it. This must have been too much for the sailors because they dove in the water as we pulled up to go over the top of the mast.'

Lieutenant Alvin Skaggs, pilot, 448th Bomb Group, Seething

CROMER

'We want to go to Cromer if it warms up and lay out in the sun on the beach since they've been cleared now of wire and mines. Might even go swimming.'

Captain Ralph H. Elliott

COASTAL LANDMARKS

'Splasher 5 at Cromer was the familiar place of assembly and return. Great Yarmouth and Lowestoft were our front doors on the North Sea. Beachy Head, Dungeness, Orfordness, Spithead, all became the familiar points from which we would depart for the enemy coast.'

Allan Healy

This is what Captain Ralph H. Elliott, pilot, 467th BG, wrote in a letter home to his wife, Vonny, during the war. Elliott added, 'Actually it was a houseboat that we poled down the waterway and managed to anchor out in the Broads for the summer And I had to carefully explain what we meant by the "Norfolk Broads" to stay out of trouble at home.'

Yvonne and I went back there in 1982; the same boat was still anchored out in the Broads in exactly the same place as we left it in 1945.

What remains of Raydon airfield today.

A SUFFOLK CHRISTMAS

'Christmas 1944 and l was in the land of Dickens - real inns, real beefsteak, real ale drawn in pewter, open fireplaces, huge old oaken beams in the smoke-seasoned rooms filled with warmth and good cheer even though the country was in its fifth year of war.

I was stationed in Knettishall, a small Suffolk village that could have come right out of the pages of Dickens or off the front of a Christmas card. It was Christmas Eve and went to St. Mary's Church, my third Christmas away from home. I felt I must be there. St. Mary's was over 500 years old - unheated except for coal stoves and unlighted except for hundreds of candles burning around the inside of the church and on the altar.

There was deep snow on the ground and lighted by the gleaming candlelight shining through the frosted, stained glass. We sang beautifully, *Silent Night, Holy Night*, in that ancient place of worship, then quietly filed out into the winter night, back to our drab, cold barracks, but with a warm glow of a beautiful Christmas celebration in our hearts. On 20 February 1945 our crew was shot down over Nuremberg and imprisoned for the duration of the war, but I had the special memory of that blessed night to carry me through the trials to come.'

Staff Sergeant Walter M. 'Boots' Mayberry,
388th Bomb Group.
All ten of 2nd Lieutenant Joseph D. Ellis
crew were taken prisoner.

A modern view towards Sudbury.

SUDBURY SOJOURN

'Sudbury's river is the Stour, pronounced "Stoor" and it is a lovely river, made justly famous by the paintings of Suffolk's two native sons, Constable and Gainsborough. From Sudbury to the sea it winds its way through a verdant valley, with rolling slopes on both sides, dotted with red-roofed villages, squat, square grey churches and the neat Suffolk fields, enclosed in their modelled hedgerows, curving up to the sky…I loved Sudbury and its people too much to stay long away and I came down to Sudbury from Honington and from Eye and from Norwich and across from Huntingdon and from Cambridge and up from Gosfield and Braintree and Birch and from Bury St. Edmunds and from Ipswich again. And occasionally I came all the way from London, to find Joan waiting at the station, with a heart-warming smile and a "Hello, Robert," in her musical voice and then we would repeat the week-ends of the past, just as if we were the only two people in the world. But as the months went by I found it harder and harder to get to Sudbury and my visits were measured by months instead of by weeks. And at the end, although our letters never stopped, I did not come back to Sudbury at all.'

Robert Arbib Jr.

PIN-UP GIRLS

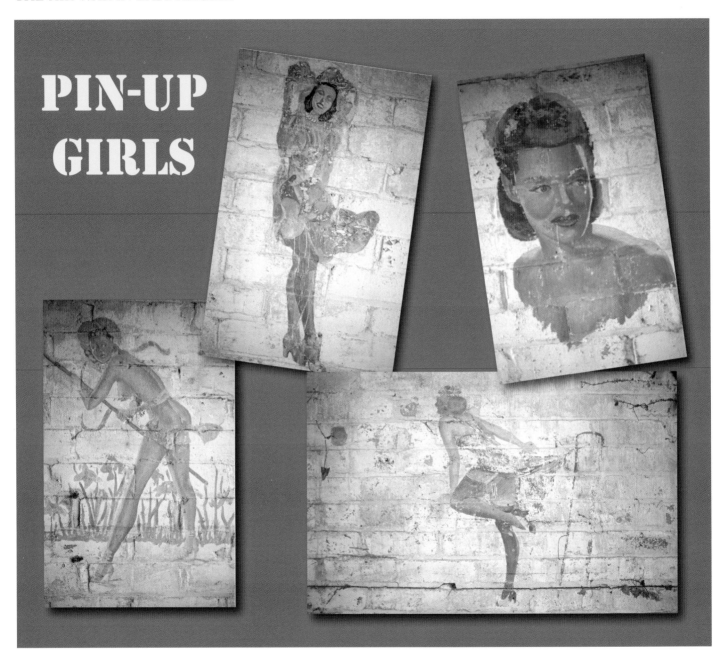

PIN-UP GIRLS

'Pin-ups proliferated with the availability of artwork by magazine artists, Alfredo Vargas, George Petty and Gil Elvegren. The artists' works appeared in monthly magazines such as *Esquire* but pin-ups in *Life* and *Saturday Evening Post* were regularly clipped out by the troops. Calendar girls were also much sought-after, usually an even dozen. Pin-up girls became commonplace features in base barbershops, crew huts and in clubs.'

Walter E. Brown MD

MY GIRL BACK HOME

'The pin-up Varga Girl in the foxhole or in the barracks represents life. She pictures to the men all that is beautiful in life. The Varga Girl tells him that there is this beauty back there in the world, the world to which he wants to return when the war is over. The Varga Girl represents his girl, his home, his family. This thought is not far-fetched. His girl back home may not be as pretty as the picture of the Varga Girl, but this does not matter. She is a symbol of his girl. If he does not have a girl of his own back home, then he thinks of the Varga Girl as his hope of finding a pretty girl…'

Chaplain James Good Brown, 381st Bomb Group, Ridgewell.

BYE BYE BABY

'Towards the end of the war Butch, who worked in the cookhouse, kindly gave me a photograph album. The two covers and the spine of the album were cut and expertly shaped with aluminium from the B-24's bomb bay doors. We then went to several Nissen huts, taking the "pin-ups" off the walls and placing them in my album, a souvenir of those dramatic days."

John Gilbert, who lived on Wendling airfield

WHEN THE LIGHTS COME ON AGAIN

'We had dinner at a restaurant near our hotel. We ordered braised beef and were given a couple of minute slices of cold corned beef. This tasty dish brought memories of the mess at Lavenham, where we were served corned beef straight from the tin at least four days a week. We pleaded piteously with the waitress not to spoil our excursion into Civvy Street with this sinister reminder of Army life, and she obligingly brought us a stew in which there were a few pieces of beef. A couple of my fellow countrymen entered with a pair of migratory working ladies. One of the Americans had a quart bottle of brandy on his hip, which was a double accomplishment, in view of the scarcity of brandy and the tightness of our uniforms. The current ideal of the well-dressed soldier was one who had to hold his breath for fear of bursting his seams. This was not

Opposite page: Pin-up pictures from the walls at Shipdham air base.

Ron Batley (left) Curator at the Thorpe Abbotts Memorial Museum points out the Courage Rooster bar tap to Mike Faley, 100th Bomb Group Historian from Studio City, California. This cast metal rooster was given to Master Sergeant Bob Spangler, a line chief in the 351st Bomb Squadron after it was 'acquired' by one of the GIs during a night out in a local pub. Bob kept it for 50 years before returning it to Thorpe Abbotts.

Post-war Picadilly.

a bad thing from the MPs point of view, for one's first impulse after downing a drink was to loosen a button here or there, which made it easy for the MPs to keep their daily quota of arrests filled.

After dinner we went to Rainbow Corner to see the GI's wound round the lamp posts and to steal some soap from the American Red Cross, for we had forgotten to bring any with us and the hotel, of course, did not provide any. The doorman stopped Bernard, but I explained that he was my guest (or should I have said accomplice?) and that we were going to stay only long enough to steal a tablet of soap. The washroom had only one piece of soap, and a very dingy one at that, and we wrapped it in a handkerchief and made off with it.

We emerged into Piccadilly and were disappointed not to find the thoroughfare thronged with the famed "Piccadilly Commandos" of whom we had heard so much. Bernard surmised that it was too early for them to have appeared yet, while I advanced the theory that it was too early for them to have appeared yet, while I advanced the theory that we probably wouldn't know one when we saw her.

Then we walked down the Mall, and suddenly the streetlights were turned on full force. It was the first time we had seen the new peacetime lighting, and we were dazzled. It may be that our eyes were made unusually sensitive by the blackout and the dim-out. At any rate, I have never seen anything so blindingly brilliant as the streetlights were that evening. We strolled about in the Park and admired Buckingham Palace in the new illumination, and then sought the luxury of our beds at the Imperial Hotel.'

20-26 July 1945, *Suffolk Summer*, John T. Appleby

LIGHTS OVER NORFOLK

Pat Everson was a 12-year old Norfolk schoolgirl at Seething and Mundham County Primary School when the 448th Bomb Group were based at Seething airfield. She has never forgotten "her" Americans. Pat has had a leading role in the Station 146 Tower Association, which has restored the control tower at Seething. Her collection of memorabilia is popular with American and English veterans alike. Here she recalls VE Day.

'I cried as they fired flares and rockets to celebrate VE Day. My mother explained they were so happy to be going home. After the war, the base was used to store bombs and in my teens, I went on the' runway to pick cowslips. The runways stretched out into the distance, so empty yet so full…I swore out loud that I would never forget them.'

RETURN VISIT

'I went back to Molesworth in the summer of 1977. It was a bleak, blustery day – one of those sudden interpolations of English weather that are so unpredictable. But the weather was entirely in keeping with my mood. English friends took us there and at first I saw nothing familiar. Then

Searchlights on Norwich Cathedral celebrating VE Day in 1945.

I saw the runways and a hangar that was still standing. There were the control tower and the water tower. I tried to find where I had lived. There was nothing but rubble. Sheep were grazing on where the 360th Squadron had lived. I thought of my friends. Of all the thousands of boys and men who were here in 1944, I was the solitary veteran of the 303rd who had come to the reunion of the Eighth Air Force.

'Here was my lost youth – where I had left it. Tears misted my eyes and I felt a great sadness. There was the Old Saxon church, still sleeping the centuries away. I thoughts of Gray's *'Elegy Written in a Country Churchyard'* and how appropriate it would have been for someone to read it on this occasion.

'There were the hardstands where had rested *Knockout Dropper, Eight Ball, The Floose* and *The Duchess*. These were the hard evidence that this incredible thing had happened. …A different kind of American had live here. Perhaps the greatest flowering of the American spirit had been reached in this place, had flourished for a short season and had subsided quickly, leaving scarcely a trace of its burgeoning.'

Ben Smith, *Chick's Crew*

In a classroom at Molesworth in the mid-1970s there was a wartime target list with rows of dates and swastikas. In another building being used as a fire section, there was a mural that was painted post war in three parts. Flanking the central design was a crouching lion and an eagle perching on the branch of a tree. Each part of the mural was beautifully detailed and coloured, particularly the three figures symbolic of the American armed forces. The installation of a false ceiling obliterated the lower part of the centrepiece showing early jet aircraft. (Steve Gotts)

Memorial at Great Ashfield commemorating those American airmen who lost their lives while stationed there during the war.

'It is logical to think that the Eighth Air Force anticipated that the 78th Fighter Group at Duxford would become a showplace…I had been stationed at Station 357 longer than I had been on any other military base since I joined the Army Air Force and it was hard to believe that I was leaving what had become more like a home than any other station that I had been. It was a place where we shared the same ideals, trials and tribulations; I couldn't help but feel like I belonged.'

Ernest E. Russell, adapted from *A Mississippi Fighter Pilot in WWII*

IN MEMORIAM

In the village churchyard of All Saints Church **Great Ashfield** is a memorial bearing the inscription: 'In memoriam of the officers and men of the 385th Heavy Bombardment Group US Army Air Force who gave their lives in the air battles over Europe 1943-1944. This plaque is placed here by the comrades of those men as an everlasting tribute to their heroic sacrifice and unselfish devotion to duty.' The plaque was sited outside the HQ building at Great Ashfield as early as 1944. A memorial altar can be found in the north aisle of the church as well as the 385th's Roll of Honour, a book containing the names of all those killed in action. A stained glass

Left: *Memorial to the 355th Fighter Group near Steeple Morden.*

Above: *Stained glass memorial window at St Catherine's Church, Litlington.*

window next to the American Memorial Altar commemorates those who lost their lives while stationed at Great Ashfield. It depicts the sky with aircraft and a dove for peace, as well as the three trees, which were the landmark on the airfield for returning aircraft.

At the side of the minor road between Litlington and Steeple Morden is the superb 355th Fighter Group memorial, made of Portland and York stone with a Mustang propeller forming an impressive centre-point. The memorial bears the badges of the 355th's three squadrons, the Second Air Scouting Force and the group crest. Inscribed are outlines of the Thunderbolt and Mustang and details of the group's units and war record, with "over 1500 enemy aircraft damaged - destroyed". In front of the memorial is a part of a large granite block from a blitzed church in London. When the runways were laid, rubble from blitzed buildings in London was used for the perimeter track and the granite block on the memorial had been used in a false fire-place in the control tower.

On Sunday 16 May 1993, the 50th anniversary of the 355th's arrival at Steeple Morden, the Bishop of Huntingdon dedicated a memorial stained glass window to the 355th Fighter Group in St. Catherine's Church, Litlington. John F. Dobbertin Jr's design shows the American eagle, wings spread over the blazing red and yellow emblem of the 355th Fighter Group with a glistening dagger streaking through the centre and there are silhouettes of the P-51 Mustang and

P-47 Thunderbolt. In May 2005 only three of the veterans made it back to Steeple Morden for the VE-Plus 60 years celebration in the church, which was covered by the BBC.

QUIDENHAM MEMORIAL

At Quidenham 1½ miles NW of Kenninghall in the 14th century chapel in the south aisle of St Andrews Church is a stained glass window showing an airman, aircraft overhead, an angel and Unit badges with the motto, 'E sempre l'ora' subscribed by personnel of 96th Bomb Group at Snetterton Heath. The preliminary design for the window was conceived and drawn up by Sergeant Gerald Athey, an aircraft mechanic at Snetterton. Mr Reginald Bell of London, much of whose work can be seen in America, including some of the windows kin the Cathedral Church of St. John the Divine, New York, designed the stained glass. The Bishop of Norwich dedicated the chapel on 17 November 1944. A service of remembrance was held in the church on 30 May 1946 in memory of the men of the 8th Air Force who were killed in WWII. The service was broadcast to the USA and Richard Dimbleby described to the people of America, the beautiful memorial, the service and the scene in the church.

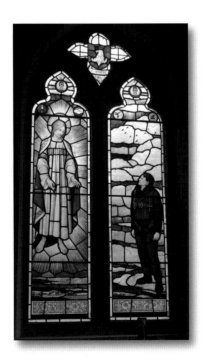

BIBLIOGRAPHY

A Thousand Destroyed, Grover C. Hall Jr.

Bomber Pilot, Philip Ardery, The University Press of Kentucky, Lexington, Kentucky, 1978.

Century Bombers: The Story of the Bloody Hundred, Richard Le Strange 100th BG Memorial Museum, 1989.

Chick's Crew: A Tale of the Eighth Air Force. Ben Smith Jr., Privately Published 1978, 1983, 2006.

The Sweet and the Sour – Beryl and the War, Bob Shaver. Privately Published

8th Air Force At War. Memories and Missions, England 1942-45. Martin W. Bowman. PSL 1994

The Eighth AF News: Journal of the Mighty Eighth. Edited by Walter E. Brown

The Fall Of The Fortresses: A personal account of one of the most daring- and deadly – air battles of the Second World War. Elmer Bendiner (Souvenir Press 1980)

The 78th Fighter Group in World War II by Garry L. Fry (Phalanx Publishing 1991).

Fields of Little America, Martin W. Bowman. Wensum Books 1977, PSL & GMS 2003.

First of the Many, Captain John R. 'Tex' McCrary and David E. Sherman. 1944.

First Over Germany: A History of the 306th Bomb Group. Russell A. Strong. 1982.

Flak at 12 O'Clock: A Teenage Kansas Farm Boy's Experiences, Dean M. Bloyd.

Here We Are Together: The Notebook of an American Soldier in Britain, Robert S. Arbib Jr, Privately Published 1945

452nd BG History

In Search of Peace, 453rd Bomb Group History. Mike Benarchik

Jonah's Feet are Dry - The Experience of the 353rd Fighter Group during World War II

Letters Home and Other Stuff, Major Ralph H. Elliott. Unpublished

Reluctant Witness: Memoirs from the last year of the European Airwar 1944-45. James J. Mahoney & Brian H. Mahoney. Trafford 2001

A Mississippi Fighter Pilot in WWII, Ernest E. Russell, Trafford Publishing 2007

Skyways to Berlin, Major John M. Redding & Captain Harold Leyshon. Bobbs Merrill, 1943.

Suffolk Summer, John T. Appleby, Privately Published 1948

The 467th Bombardment Group, Allan Healy. Privately Printed 1947.

The Route As Briefed. The History of the 92nd Bombardment Group USAAF 1942-45. John S. Sloan.

Three Years in the Army Air Forces. A WW2 Narrative, Staff Sergeant Dale R. VanBlair

"There we were…or The saga of crew No. 8. Ronald D. Spencer

Yank Magazine